"Sahar was a great success at our workshop in Stockholm. The result was fantastic and hit all the right notes."

— IKEA

"You were mindblowingly marvellous."

— Innotown Norway

"Your energising talk on the necessity of passion to drive business growth was inspiring for everyone… I overheard the audience quoting 'Leap and the net will appear' for days afterward! Needless to say, our expectations were surpassed."

— Infosys

Praise for Anyone Can Do It
by Sahar and Bobby Hashemi

"I welcome this refreshingly honest and insightful book which lifts the lid on what it takes to be a successful entreprenuer, and explains what its like to dream a market."

— Martin Wyn Griffith
Chief Executive BERR Enterprise Directorate

"A great success story and an inspirational role model for entrepreneurs in all business sectors... Books such as this illustrate not only the 'nuts and bolts' of entrepreneurialism, but also give invaluable access to the experience of others."

— Andrew Main Wilson
Chief Operating Officer of Institute of Directors

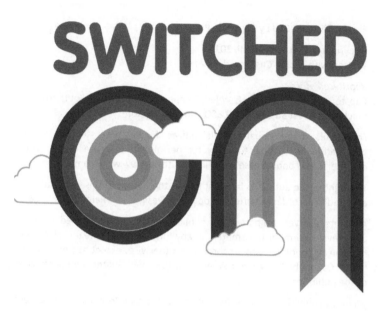

SWITCHED ON

Sahar Hasher

CAPSTON
be inspired

First published 2010 by Capstone Publishing Ltd (a Wiley Company)

Registered office
Capstone Publishing Ltd. (A Wiley Company), The Atrium, Southern Gate, Chichester, West Sussex, PO19 8SQ, United Kingdom

For details of our global editorial offices, for customer services and for information about how to apply for permission to reuse the copyright material in this book please see our website at www.wiley.com.

Library of Congress Cataloguing-in-Publication Data

978 1 9064 6583 4

A catalogue record for this book is available from the British Library.

Set in 12.5 on 14.5pt Calibri by Aptara
Printed and Bound by T.J. International Ltd, Padstow, Cornwall

This book is dedicated
to my mother
'everything I do, is your doing'
ee cummings

and

to my husband,
James

All of us, whether or not we are warriors, have a cubic centimetre of chance that pops out in front of our eyes from time to time. The difference between an average man and a warrior is that the warrior is aware of his, and one of his tasks is to be alert, deliberately waiting, so that when his cubic centimetre of chance pops out he has the necessary speed, the prowess, to pick it up.

— Carlos Castaneda

Contents

A Letter from the Author

"I tap dance to work."

Warren Buffett

Do you?

Or do you read this and think, "No wonder he tap dances to work. He's Warren Buffett. Everything he touches turns to gold. It's a no-brainer. So would you if you had that much in the bank."

But that's not why he does it. Sure, we all come to work to earn money, but there needs to be something more, much much more.

And that something more is what this book about is. Because being at work is about more than just the pay cheque.

Work is about fulfilment, it's about engaging your mind and nourishing your soul. Work is an enormous part of your life, so just turning up is no longer an option. The adage that you leave your personality at the door when you go to work is outdated, gone. If work is such a large part of your life, you'll want to live it well.

Switched On is about being awake to what you do and feeling energized by it. Why? Because it engages your interest and stimulates your creativity. Working in a switched-on way will, by definition, make you great at what you do. It will generate the plaudits and rewards and make you valued and indispensable in the organization you work for.

What *Switched On* is not about is going to work on autopilot. Ever feel that your mind is so much elsewhere that you barely remember the journey into work? Somehow you just arrived ... Then eight hours later you left again. Nothing revved you up, there was nothing remarkable about your day. I'd say you were living for the weekend, but I'd hardly call it living. You're merely ticking over.

Living and making a living should be the same thing. That's what being switched on is all about. It's about leaving your comfort zone for a more enthralling, fulfilling journey, packed with rich experiences. Leaving your comfort zone is not about quitting your job, it's about leaving behind the complacency of the comfort zone. It's about switching on to the potential in front of you and grabbing it with both hands. It's about using the comfort zone for its comforts, not its straightjacket.

How do I know this? Because I've been both "switched on" and "switched off" at work. I've been a grey-faced automaton in work mode, where I've left my personality at the door as I've entered the office every day. I've felt the frustration and emptiness of being disconnected from what I do.

But I pushed myself past the threshold of my comfort zone and took a leap into a life where "work" was not the antidote to "life" but a wonderful, expanding, reinforcing part of it. A life where "work" and "fun" are not opposite words.

Switched On is about adopting some habits that will change your life at work. Because, let's face it, we're at work for most of our waking hours if we're honest, so we should be enjoying every minute of it.

I called this book *Switched On* because there's a natural tendency within the traditional working environment to accept the status quo. It's not that you are switched *off* as such, simply that corporate culture seems to encourage just going with the flow. But why go with the flow when something as simple as switching on to a few easy habits could revive your working life, making it so much more?

This even affects your competitive advantage as an employee. Think about it. Today's working world has computing technology, international outsourcing and every resource – including human – available faster, cheaper and better somewhere else. What is your point of differentiation? You need to up your game.

And it's easy to do. You've already been using all the skills you need, just not all of them at work. You need to package up everything you do – at home, at work and at play – and bring it all into your life at work. By bringing 100% of yourself, no one else can match it.

I believe anyone can switch on, that is why I have written this book. *Switched On* isn't about finding something new. It's about shaking off old constraints and digging deep within yourself to find resources that you have always had. All you need to do is wake them up and turn them on.

In the words of Joseph Campbell:

You want to put yourself on a kind of track that has been there all the while, waiting for you, and the life that you ought to be living is the one you are living now.

— Joseph Campbell, quoted in Joseph Jaworski,
Synchronity, 1996

Living the life I ought to be living is something I have always wished for myself – and I wish it for you too.

— Sahar, London, March 2010

And the day came when the risk to remain tight in the bud was more painful than the risk to blossom.

— Anaïs Nin, Risk

What Does Being Switched On Mean?

Becoming Switched On is a shift

from ...	to ...
Doing just enough	... giving 100%
Just hanging on to your job	... growing and learning every day
Standing still	... being on an enthralling journey
Always waiting to be told what to do next	... being proactive
Being bored doing meaningless work	... feeling fulfilled and inspired
Being complacent in your comfort zone	... honing your creative skills
Being seen as just OK	... being indispensable

The 8 Habits of a Switched-On Mindset

Switched On is a mindset. A mindset is the by-product of a set of behaviours. And behaviours you *can* change.

It's simply a question of adopting new habits. I have learned these habits in my working life. Through starting my own businesses I have developed a mindset typical of entrepreneurs. But this "entrepreneurial mindset" is not limited to entrepreneurs. Certainly, the habits have their roots there, but their application is so much wider.

I have realized that the most productive mindset comes when you are totally switched on to what you do every day. It's the backbone behind your persistence, the inspiration for your creativity and the motivation always, always to keep moving forwards.

The entrepreneurial mindset becomes the Switched On mindset.

So the eight habits in this book are based on the habits of an entrepreneur. They are about acting small and being nimble, however big the organization is. Companies can give you the freedom you need to unleash your whole being, but you will often need to work at doing so. The strength, resources and security of the corporate umbrella used with the new Switched On mindset brought about by these eight habits can help you to achieve great success.

Habit 1: Believing anyone can do it.
You already have all the tools you need to be switched on. You have probably used them before, but by virtue of the daily grind they've become a bit rusty. You need to get them oiled again.

Habit 2: Putting yourself in your customer's shoes.
To regain a perspective on the true purpose of what you do, you need to look at what you mean to customers. Whoever they may be, reconnecting with the impact of what you do brings your job to life.

Habit 3: Getting out of the office with your light switched on.
Opening yourself up to the world beyond company walls removes any blinkers. With a wider focus you receive so much stimulation it can't help but boost your motivation and energy.

Habit 4: Being clueless.
If you're going to get out of the rut, away from the daily grind and turn off the autopilot, you need to

make a break with the past. Processes, systems and a "how we've always done it" mentality will only hold you back.

Habit 5: Prototyping.
The four steps thus far may have fired you up to great new ideas and creativity, but it's all for naught if you can't bring them to life. Before they have a chance to fly away, grab those ideas and make them real. Start small and keep experimenting under the radar until you get it right.

Habit 6: Notching up nos.
Overcome the endemic fear of failure in institutions. Resistance is an integral part of trial and error, and trial and error are key parts of seizing opportunities.

Habit 7: Bootstrapping.
Bureaucracy creates bottlenecks for implementing new ideas. They can't go down conventional channels. You need to be creative in making them happen. This chapter helps you break down the corporate barriers and execute your ideas, however limited your resources.

Habit 8: Take 100% of yourself to work.
You don't need to suppress part of yourself to be professional at work. The barriers between work and play are imaginary. You can't afford to leave part of yourself behind when you're in "work"

mode. The new era demands you take your heart as well as your head to work.

As with any habit, your effectiveness at being switched on develops over time. The more you get into the habits of switched-on behaviour, the more you reinforce it and strengthen it so it becomes second nature, a natural and intuitive part of everything you do.

And, like laughter and enthusiasm, it's infectious. By becoming Switched On you inspire all those around you – colleagues, partners, friends – and they can't help but join in. So take the leap.

"Leap and the net will appear."

That's my motto in life.

Habit 1

Believing Anyone Can Do It

The question is not "Do I have it in me?" but "How do I switch it on?"
It's about using the fundamental human abilities of everyday life in our life at work

know what you're going to say. One of two things. Either:

This isn't me.

Or

My company won't go with it.

This chapter is about getting over these two – altogether imaginary – hurdles and changing your frames of reference. But before that, we need to tackle some mental blocks that might be hindering you.

Mental block 1: I haven't got it in me

The first block is thinking that you haven't got the ability. That you need some special chromosome or magic dust infused in your DNA. But this kind of behaviour isn't using anything special. You do already have it in you. The essence of being switched on is opening up your creativity.

What do I mean by creativity? Creativity is not finding the next great idea. It's not restricted to a marketing department or research and development team. Every element of your working life requires creativity whether you're aware of it or not. It's about problem solving, interacting with customers or simply talking to colleagues. You can be a creative accountant, a creative secretary, a creative police officer – when you go beyond your job remit.

Being switched on is about not *just* doing your job. A lawyer who only drafts documents is just doing a job. A switched-on lawyer suggests creative ways for you to do the deal, making it more advantageous for you.

Creativity is about exploring different ways in which you can do something, however mundane. It's about making yourself aware of the things around you and what you can be doing to improve them – continually reinventing and renewing.

In essence, creativity is a tool you often use in your everyday life outside work. You just need to learn to use it more in your working life.

All it takes is a bit of rewiring of your brain. You may think that you are past that, and that any change in habit is difficult to achieve after doing something the same way for so long.

In the *New York Times* bestseller *The Plastic Mind*, science journalist Sharon Begley explains that contrary to what scientists traditionally thought, the hard-wired brain can be rewired long into adulthood and retains much of the plasticity of the developing brain. She says: "The actions we take can literally expand or contract different regions of the brain, pour more juice into quiet circuits and dampen down activity in buzzing ones."

So there you have it. It's never too late to change a habit. Like any muscle you haven't used in a while, your brain and the creative part of it just need some gentle flexing again. You *can* become switched on if you really set your mind to it for long enough.

Mental block 2: The comfort zone

By definition, the more comfortable the company is, the more it stifles individuality and creativity. Start-ups and smaller companies are in a healthy state of discomfort. They have nothing to rely on but their people's gut instinct, energy and creativity. But as a business gets bigger, the discipline and structure it needs put into place a certain amount of routine and complacency, which unfortunately stifle creativity.

This isn't your fault. It's a natural by-product of the comfort zone. Historically, small companies started off agile and entrepreneurial – because they had to be. But when they grew to become big and successful they could afford to stay just that – big. And as their success continued they became like huge oil tankers – unable to turn around or change course. This wasn't a problem when the pace of change was slower, as companies could afford to take time making decisions and doing things in the same way they had always been done.

Today, however, the world moves much faster and simply maintaining the status quo isn't good enough.

In this world of huge uncertainty, no company can survive by relying on what it's done before. What makes money now isn't necessarily going to continue to make money in the future. Therefore every company needs to explore new possibilities on a continual basis. And they need the ideas and opportunity spotting to come from you. It's no longer enough for you to churn out yet another standardized product. The future belongs to companies that, while being well established, are very, very agile. They need a constant flow of new ideas about different ways of doing things. They need small, incremental innovations *all the time*.

You need to see the comfort zone as an illusion – it no longer exists. By moving out of the comfort zone you're helping your company to continually renew and reinvent itself and you're helping yourself become part of the new world.

If I stand in the sand and draw a circle around myself I am in my comfort zone. Now I step outside and I feel fear, and today I know that that is a good place to be. When I stay there for a while I become familiar and the fear subsides. Now I can draw a wider circle around myself and my comfort zone gets larger.

— Simon Woodroffe, The Book of Yo! 2000

Mental block 3: Self-belief

To go on the journey, you need self-belief. That's a frightening concept for some people, who believe that self-belief is something you either have or haven't got. That you're either 100% confident or not at all. Thankfully, this isn't the case.

Self-belief is something we've all got – it's just that some of us may not be using it enough. It isn't true that some people are born with minimal self-belief and others are endowed with soaring confidence and belief that they can do anything. But self-belief is something that you need to nurture and foster. It's a by-product of your behaviours and actions. And it will grow exponentially as you start out on your new journey to becoming switched on. You just need to dip your toe in the water.

The journey of a thousand miles begins with a single step.

— Lao-Tzu

Begin by taking the first step towards changing your behaviour and your self-belief and commitment, which may well be non-existent at the beginning, will grow along the journey.

At some point you will look back and be amazed at the paradigm shift that has taken place, and see the world of difference between yourself now and what you were like before you started. This new-found self-belief feeds into a virtuous, self-perpetuating circle and the momentum builds to drive you forward towards becoming more and more switched on.

Concerning all acts of initiative (and creation), there is one elementary truth, the ignorance of which kills countless ideas and splendid plans: that the moment one definitely commits oneself, then providence moves too.

All sorts of things occur to help one that would never otherwise have occurred. A whole stream of events issues from the decision, raising in one's favour all manner of unforeseen events, meetings and material assistance, which no man could have dreamt would have come his way.

— W N Murray, The Scottish Himalayan Expedition

Mental block 4: You can't change company culture

Now that you can see how to overcome your own blocks to becoming more switched on, you are probably turning to concerns that are bigger than you. What if my company doesn't "get" this? What if the business suppresses it? It's all very well turning around one person – but a whole organization?

You're not the only one to have these doubts. "My company's culture is not conducive to this" is a common gripe among individuals.

But what makes up your organization's culture? It's surely not written in a constitution. The organizational culture is simply made up of the beliefs, attitudes and behaviours of the people who work there.

But if you start thinking and behaving differently, it will be infectious. The momentum and energy you create will quickly spread around your office. Switched-on thinking liberates you from the corporate straightjacket and your positive, authentic energy will attract others. More and more individuals will take it on board and slowly the whole organization will begin to feel the buzz in one way or another. It's inevitable.

If you cut a blade of grass, you shake the universe.

— Chinese proverb

Practice makes perfect

Do you know the 99% perspiration, 1% inspiration rule? Perhaps when you first saw this book you thought it was going to be all in the mind. Not at all: becoming switched on is utterly practical. It's a direct by-product of your actions. And like succeeding with anything practical, you need to practise, practise, practise.

People love to subscribe to the idea of overnight success. The thought that someone was in the right place at the right time and that's all it took. That it was effortless and instant. But in pursuit of the fairytale ending, the whole truth is often glossed over. People so often "forget" about the long years of hard, mind-numbing dross before the infamous "night before".

In *Outliers* Malcolm Gladwell talks about The Beatles' path to success. He pointed out that the band had performed live 1200 times before they seemingly burst onto the pop scene. Most bands don't play live 1200 times in their whole careers.

The point is that you should not be put off by others' seemingly effortless success or let it be a barrier to you beginning the Switched On journey. Like a swan gliding serenely on the top of the water, there's an awful lot of frantic paddling below the surface.

Think of it this way: it can take 15 years to become an overnight success!

Your USP: Right-brain thinking

It's worth thinking for a moment about how creativity works. The brain is divided into two hemispheres. The left brain is the logical, analytical, computer-like side. It prefers what it knows already: the logical and the routine. And the right brain is the intuitive, big picture and creative side.

It's interesting to see how much of our working life we operate primarily through the left side. We don't use intuitive, right-brain thinking enough.

And yet the right brain is where the magic lies. It engages you emotionally with what you do. It brings you empathy, intuition and individuality. Yet in the world of work it's traditionally been considered to be too flaky and frivolous to use. Until now.

In his bestselling book *A Whole Mind: Why Right Brainers Will Rule the Future*, Daniel Pink talks about the two forces that are making our left-brain capabilities increasingly obsolete in business. The first is outsourcing. The fact that someone abroad can do a job equally well but for less money than you can means that these days companies are not looking so much for left-brain workers. This is the stuff they can get done elsewhere. But what they can't outsource is your creativity, your empathy with customers, your playfulness, your big-picture thinking and all the other habits this book is about.

The second force that Pink identifies is computers. They can essentially replace and do much faster the routine, standardized work that humans used to do.

So increasingly you need to focus your efforts on what foreign workers can't do cheaper and computers can't do faster. And that's why using your right brain becomes increasingly important in the world of business.

Your unique selling point (USP) resides in your right brain. And the best part of this is that right-brain thinking is a human capacity that everyone has, something that anyone can tap into. Some people use right-brain skills in day-to-day life and not at work, and some don't use them at all. If that's the case, it's just a question of getting the right-brain muscles back into shape and making a habit of using them.

Press the delete/mute button

As human beings our minds are continually in overdrive. We have about 70,000 thoughts a day. We spend a surprising amount of time in an internal dialogue – in other words, we are very busy having a conversation with ourselves!

Our moods and performance can often depend on whether this self-talk is positive or negative.

Whenever I want to do something new or different, there's always a little voice in my head, an incessant chatter, somehow sabotaging it, telling me not to go for it. That voice is often negative, as it's bombarded with all the dreary news and events that come in from the outside world and feeds them back into my subconscious as anxiety and fear,

The only solution I've found to quieten this negative voice is to press the "mute" button. Unless you consciously press "mute" – or even "delete", to get rid of it altogether – this incessant stream of negative thoughts will paralyse you rather than push you ahead.

This is what all great athletes do. As we already know, a big part of their training is not merely physical, but mental. They learn to control their inner voice, "almost like an MP3 player of positive affirmations that they play over and over, increasing the volume and intensity"[*].

So you see, this is not a whole new set of skills. It's just a question of changing your habits and tapping into what you've already got within you.

---

[*] Raisethebar.co.uk

Takeaways

- Switched On is not a personality type, it's a behaviour

- Consciously take yourself out of your comfort zone

- Creativity is not intuitive – you can develop and practise it

- Don't ask yourself "Am I creative?" Ask "How can I unblock my creativity?"

- Moving out of your comfort zone ignites your creativity

- You build up self-belief with your actions

- An extra 1% self-belief every day gets you almost 100% in three months

- Focus on what you can control – your own habits

- Bring your whole persona to work

- Press the mute button on your doubts

- Remember that FEAR is False Evidence Appearing Real

Habit 2

Putting Yourself in Your Customers' Shoes

Make an emotional connection with your customer. Putting the customer (and not your boss) at the centre of your world gives you a more meaningful motivation than just coming in for the pay cheque. Empathy is putting yourself in the customer's shoes and experiencing the world from their perspective

These must be the world's most overused business clichés: *customer focus, the customer is king, putting the customer at the centre*. Are you stifling a yawn?

It's difficult to write a chapter on customer focus while keeping a straight face. The number of mission statements that trumpet *a passion for customers* is not worth guessing. And they're usually the ones from companies with abominable customer service.

But without empathy, these are merely empty declarations of devotion to the customer.

Yes, the customer is absolutely the most important reason you are there, doing the job you are doing, but putting them on a pedestal and worshipping them from afar isn't what turns you on to your role.

Becoming your customers is another story.

Being switched on is the polar opposite of "us" the company and "them" the customer mentality, which almost overlooks the fact that its customers are fellow human beings.

Being switched on is about remembering that customers are real people, like you and me. They are not simply a market segment with predefined behavioural patterns. It's important really to get inside their skin.

Seeing the world from the perspective of the person on the receiving end of what you do gives meaning and purpose to what you do. It reignites your enthusiasm and gets you out of autopilot and into a switched-on frame of mind.

That's why it is useless repeating this particular "c" word again and again when there is a fundamental disconnect between the world of the company and its customers outside.

The ivory tower analogy is no joke – is it any coincidence that top management is often on the top floor? That's physically about as far away from customers as you can get.

The more disconnected you become from the customer, the harder it is to empathise with the people who are buying your product or service, and therefore the harder it is to get inspired and make the crucial emotional connection with what you do.

It's so easy to lose sight of the customer and instead rely merely on facts and figures. Methodical, perhaps, but inspirational? Without boosting your power of empathy, you lose sight of your customers and see only statistics.

To get switched on and become fulfilled by what you do, you need to reconnect wholeheartedly with the world of the customer rather than merely pay lip service to them. The benefit of this is not only that you will do better in your career, but that you will enjoy it much, much more.

By using your heart as well as your mind, you are able to engage emotionally with your work.

Even if you have no interaction with the customer side of your organization, it's still crucial that you understand what role you play in their world. How can you possibly get any personal satisfaction from the job you do if you don't or can't see the end result it contributes towards? If you see the end consumer as nothing more than a market segment, on a personal level you will feel only the emptiness that comes from doing meaningless work.

Think back to front: See yourself as the customer, not the "seller"

Will King, the founder of shaving and skincare brand King of Shaves, always had trouble shaving. He had sensitive skin and routinely got a rash from using standard foam shaving cream. He tells the story that one morning his girlfriend got him to try oil on his skin before shaving, to see if it made any difference. He found it worked and so started bottling the product in his bathroom. His attitude was: "If this works for me, it will work for other people."

King started his business from a personal unmet need. This is a common entrepreneurial trait. I've also started businesses because I was the customer for what they were offering. In fact, I can't even envisage how it's possible to work somewhere and not be a customer.

I started Skinny Candy because I love sweets and chocolate and yet feel guilt pangs whenever I eat them. So I came up with the idea of a guilt-free sweets brand. Before that I started Coffee Republic, the idea for which came because I missed the skinny lattes I had got hooked on during a trip to New York, and I couldn't understand why we didn't have them in the UK. I remember mentioning casually to my brother over a family meal how much I missed the NY-style coffee bars, and he had the "light-bulb" moment many entrepreneurs talk about.

My brother said to me: "You know what? We should bring NY-style coffee bars to the UK." But my reaction was: "I'm only a customer. Why won't someone else do it and I will happily be a customer of it?"

That was the moment I realized that at that time I thought there was a fundamental disconnect between the customer and the seller. I hadn't appreciated that being the customer in a business was the most valuable position to be in.

Fast forward a few years: the coffee business we founded had become bigger and we had begun to build an organizational structure. Naturally, as the company got bigger the focus began to turn inwards, towards what was happening internally rather than externally in the world of the customer. For me as the founder, it was shocking to see how having a more formal structure with lines of reporting and processes can so easily start to disconnect you from the customer.

And the more disconnected you are, the harder it is to empathize.

This habit of always trying to be your own customer and having the mentality of "If it works for me it will work for other people" adapts just as well for any role in an organization. It's simply a question of reminding yourself every day what impact your work will have on the person at the receiving end. What are they expecting, hoping or needing to receive? Is it a product? A service? Advice? Care? An experience? Maybe it's all of these.

The best way to do this is to ask yourself: "If I were the customer, standing in their shoes, buying or paying for this product or service, what would I hope, expect or need to receive?"

It is likely that you will see that there is a disparity between what you think you are selling and what the customer is actually buying.

Buy your product, or experience your service, as the customer would. Put yourself through their experience from beginning to end. As you do this, keep thinking about ways in which you could improve the performance of the product or the experience of the service you are getting.

There's no role in which this can't be done. For example, if you are a high-street bank manager, how about actually trying to get a loan from your own branch — use a pseudonym if necessary.

Use any way that enables you to find out for yourself how your service feels to your customer. If you work in a call centre, how many times have you called up your own call centre as a bona fide customer? Feel the frustration (or the joy) the customer feels when they ring up.

Or eavesdrop on your customers, observe them very closely, watch every movement, every hesitation. At IKEA staff seek such an intimate understanding of the customer that they call it having "pillow talk" knowledge of them.

Magnus Brehmer, Marketing Specialist at Inter IKEA Systems, says: "We encourage our people to get to know the consumers in their markets, as well as they know their own life partners! Knowledge that anyone can read in demographic reports is no longer enough. We need to understand the needs and dreams they have and then ask ourselves how we can work those insights into our whole mix."

Jeff Bezos of Amazon ups it one level and talks about *"obsessing"* over customers.

Empathy is feeling with someone else, sensing what it would be like to be that person. Empathy is a stunning act of derring-do, the ultimate virtual reality – climbing into another person's mind to experience the world from that person's perspective.

— Daniel H Pink, A Whole New Mind, 2006

Think subjectively

One of the reasons IKEA is so customer-centric is the way its eccentric Ingvar Kamprad puts himself into customers' shoes, forcing himself to think subjectively rather than objectively.

He plays a game. He visits IKEA stores regularly, reinventing himself each time as different fictitious customers. In his head he is a single mother of two one day, a student fitting out his digs the next, and a newly married couple setting up home the next.

He actually purchases every item that kind of person would need. That is the only way for him to find out if these imaginary customers have everything they could want at his store.

You may think this sounds too subjective to apply to your role. Because corporate life is all about covering your actions, about checks and balances, about the collective rather than the individual. You're not trusted to rely on intuition. But I can't see why you shouldn't.

There should be a balance between playing safe and trusting your instincts. Thinking subjectively by listening to your own reactions gives you valuable insights into what you can do better, and therefore improves your performance and gives you a competitive advantage over others. It will ignite your intuition as well as channel it in the right direction.

In designing the ultimate yuppie car, what did Toyota do? It sent the Japanese design team to live like yuppies in California. Only by actually living like yuppies, with the same routines and the same needs, could they ever design a car for yuppies. After all, how could a suited and booted, nine-to-five Japanese designer create a car for a free-loving, free-living Californian without sampling the sunshine state for themselves?

Don't rely on customer surveys

We all use and enjoy products that we would not have said we wanted or needed if they had been described to us in a customer survey questionnaire.

It's a big misconception that you can connect with customers through conventional customer surveys and focus groups.

If I'd asked my customers what they wanted they would have said a faster horse.

— Henry Ford

Customer surveys are useful historically, when you want to make sure that what you already do you are doing well. They are a useful opportunity for customers to give feedback, but they are unlikely to give you any new insights or predict any new products or innovations. Customers can't tell you what they're missing.

Take the iPod as an example. Since its launch in 2001, around 200 million people have bought one. Owners of iPods love them and couldn't be without them. But if Steve Jobs had done a survey, do you think customers would have told him to invent a portable music player that you download music to from your computer?

Customers are not very imaginative or innovative. They are actually quite conservative and often reject innovations at first sight. They function well as rear-view mirrors, but are notoriously bad at predicting new products to meet their needs.

The onus rests with you to try to think the unthinkable. You need to improve your product or service beyond what they could possibly imagine. It's for you to anticipate a future need of which customers are not even aware.

Marketing is giving people things they don't even know they want yet.

— Yves Saint Laurent

An even more crucial consideration is that customer survey results can even be wrong. If you ask someone about something new or different, the most frequent response is that they don't need it. This is often because they are simply not used to it. But this isn't to say that the proposed product or service is a bad idea.

Take the customer survey that 3M's marketers carried out on the Post-it note. The results showed that the most common reaction was to ask what the point was of stickiness on the back of paper when paperclips and staples already existed. The customer surveys rejected the Post-it note idea.

For those of you who don't know the Post-it story, it's worth mentioning it here. Art Fry, the creator of the Post-it note, had come up with the idea in a rather unusual way. His colleague Dr Spencer Silver, a scientist for the technology company 3M, was trying to formulate its strongest glue yet. Perversely, he wound up with one that was even weaker than everything the company already made. It would stick to things, but you could peel it right off again. With an inkling that this might be useful for something, Silver kept hold of the glueless glue. It was some years later when Fry, who was continually frustrated by his bookmark dropping out of his hymnbook at church, slapped on a bit of Silver's glue to get the bookmark to stick. It stuck, but not enough to damage the pages when it was taken out again.

So Fry was his own first customer. When he came to develop his idea and launch the Post-it note, he persevered regardless of the survey results, because he had already bought into it.

When I was opening one of UK's first US-style coffee bars, if I'd asked potential customers whether or not they fancied a half-caff, skinny vanilla latte, I'm sure the most I would have got as a reaction would have been a confused stare and "No thanks, just white will do".

Steve Jobs in an interview with *Fortune*, in March 2008, says the reason iTunes was made was because the team that worked on it were its first customers. They loved music and were frustrated at not being able to carry their music libraries around with them. So they worked hard to build iTunes because they all wanted one for themselves.

It's not about convincing people that they want something they don't. We figure out what we want. And I think we're pretty good at having the right discipline to think through whether a lot of other people are going to want it, too. That's what we get paid to do.

— Steve Jobs

As well as feedback from customer surveys on new products, be wary of the reactions of colleagues in other departments who claim to represent the customers' views. People's default position tends to be to reject the unfamiliar, so colleagues' reactions to a new idea can often be misleading.

And this is why standing in customers' shoes and seeing the world from their perspective is better than just relying on their feedback or reaction.

Think of what you're doing as problem solving – it's more exciting!

People walk around being annoyed at awkward things, things they can't find, not realizing in fact they are being presented with a buffet of ideas in waiting.

Whenever you say to yourself that you are annoyed by something you should say to yourself "I wonder if there is a better way?"

And in that lies the genesis of most ideas. Almost all great ideas come from transforming a problem into a solution. As soon as you start looking at all the problems in life as opportunities then you will find yourself with many potential ideas to choose from.

— Doug Richard

If you stand in your customers' shoes you will get insight into headaches and problems that are begging to be solved. There is huge satisfaction in getting your teeth into something, getting close to the issue and problem solving. If you're far away from the customers and what they really, really want, work is only a daily slog.

Take Bill George, Harvard Business School lecturer, who as CEO of Medtronic, a medical instruments company, took the company from a market cap of $1.1 billion to $60 billion in 10 years. He knew nothing about medical instruments when he joined. So how did he get under his customers' skin? Almost literally, as it happens. He attended 120 operations where surgeons were using the companys' medical instruments.

George was in an angioplasty (surgery to repair blood vessels) when the instrument fell apart in the doctor's hands as he was threading through the patient's arteries. George commented in his book *Authentic Leadership*, "The doctor was so angry that he took the catheter covered in blood and threw it at me." After that operation, the sales rep told George that this had happened several times and he had reported it, but had never heard back from the company. George added: "As well intentioned as they were engineers were not spending time with customers and were insulated from product problems."

The sales reps had to go through seven layers of management to get to the engineers, so the latter had no idea what the faults in their products were and no opportunities to fix them. Imagine how much less frustrating and more meaningful it would be for them to have been in the operating theatre seeing what goes wrong and then being the ones to fix it.

Instead of sitting at a workshop bench with a pile of metal on one side and a sheaf of notes on the other, they would have come back to their desks with the sights, smells and sounds of a life-saving operation. They would have a greater insight into the problems that were crying out to be solved. They would have been able to improve both their own and the company's performance.

Think of it as removing an irritant

The fact is if something irritates you it is a pretty good indication that there are other people who feel the same. Irritation is a great source of energy and creativity. It leads to dissatisfaction and should prompt you to begin asking yourself the types of question that can lead to a good business idea.

— Anita Roddick

As you get into the habit of becoming closer to your customer, you'll start to notice things about your company that may have been below your radar before. And it won't be because you've started paying more attention to the customer feedback forms.

You'll start noticing these things instinctively. Why? Because with your new switched-on mindset, they'll start to irritate you. And you'll want to do something about them.

Because you'll be more sensitive to the things that might irritate the customer, you'll also be hyper-aware of the internal processes that just aren't right. These are things that before, you let slip by. You consigned them to the "necessary evil" file. They were fodder for your daily whinge by the watercooler.

When you become engaged you also become empowered. You don't feel the need to accept the status quo and you can set about putting things right. Irritants are good things. A grain of sand is an irritant; eventually it becomes a pearl.

And irritants don't just galvanize you into action to deal with the negative. They spur on creativity – an absolutely crucial element of the switched-on state of mind. As the saying goes, "Necessity is the mother of invention."

Fred Smith, founder of FedEx, got his idea for a courier company after being "infuriated" trying to get spare parts from around the US for his first business venture. FedEx was his way of removing this irritant.

Mark Zuckerberg, a student at Harvard University, noticed that the campus was crying out for a way to get to know people in different houses: "Everyone's been talking a lot about a universal face book within

Harvard," Zuckerberg told the *Harvard Crimson*. "I think it's kind of silly that it would take the university a couple of years to get around to it. I can do it better than they can, and I can do it in a week." That was in 2004, when a small computer program called "the face book" was launched among a couple of hundred university students. The rest is history.

By getting into your customers' minds and experiencing the world through their eyes, you will have a clear view of their irritants. By taking these and being innovative in your suggestions or ideas for solving them, you give yourself a huge head start in your role.

Make it personal

Back-to-front thinking, problem solving and removing irritants all come down to one thing: making it personal, making all that you do in your job *real*.

A "them" and "us" mentality makes you believe that customers aren't real, almost not human. When you read their behaviour via customer segmentation reports, behavioural pattern analysis or whatever the current fad is, you stop connecting to them as one human to another.

It's this mentality, not your job, that turns you into an automaton and ultimately "switches you off". To be switched on you need to view your relationship with your customers – however distant they may be from the work you do – as a personal one.

You do team bonding with your colleagues within the organization. You take your boss and his wife out to dinner to get to know them better on a personal level, in the hope that this will foster a better working relationship.

But what kind of bonding happens in the outside world, where your customers are?

The human resources department takes care of the personal connection between you and your colleagues, arranging the Christmas party and weekends away on activity courses. But the real customers, the ones who pay your salaries – where's their invite?

You could all be sitting round the campfire singing "Kumbaya Customer", dedicating love songs to your passionate relationship with those who consume your products or services, but unless they're leading the singing and tugging on your heart strings, the whole thing's a bit out of tune.

You see, however much you put the name of the customer and the word "passion" in neon lights on the stage at your corporate conference, it's no use unless the customer is there too, telling their stories, talking about how what *you* do affects *them*, interacting with you on a human level, face to face.

Some companies do invite customers to their conferences to recount how they interact with what the company does and how it affects their lives. This face-to-face storytelling can have a very real impact on the motivation and sense of purpose within the company.

On several occasions I've done work with police forces around the country, and I've never ceased to be surprised by how unaware they are of the true purpose of what they do. They don't really appreciate the benefit they bring to the ultimate user – the man or woman in the street.

I extol the philosophy of *Anyone Can Do It* because I am lucky to live in a country where I can walk down the street, free to feel safe and do what I love doing – and the work of the police has a lot to do with that.

But they don't necessarily see this positive difference they make. It astounds me that the bureaucracy and emphasis on what they don't do right have so disconnected them. When reminded who their "customer" is and what a positive impact they can have, they begin to feel a sense of purpose again, and a sense of pride in the achievements that do go well.

It's the same with the NHS. In my recent work with different sections of the health service, many people need to be reminded that their purpose is to save lives and that the job they do is eminently worthwhile and appreciated by their "customers".

From nurses to IT technicians, they are so wrapped up in organizational issues and problems that they forget about the true impact they have on the ultimate recipients of their services. They forget that, directly or indirectly, they save lives every day.

In both cases these people have lost the vital emotional connection that gives meaning to their working lives.

Takeaways

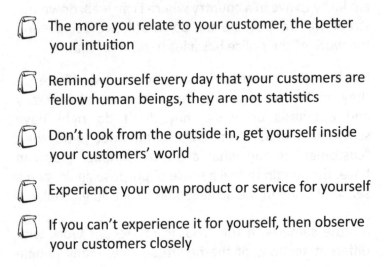

The more you relate to your customer, the better your intuition

Remind yourself every day that your customers are fellow human beings, they are not statistics

Don't look from the outside in, get yourself inside your customers' world

Experience your own product or service for yourself

If you can't experience it for yourself, then observe your customers closely

Invite customers into your world

Don't rely on surveys, remember that your task is to give customers something they yet don't know they want!

Keep asking yourself *as a customer* "Would I like this?" (instead of "Would the customer like this?")

How switched on you are is in direct proportion to how snugly your customer's shoe fits!

Habit 3

Getting Out of the Office

Creativity is borne of inspiration and perspiration – neither of which you'll find sitting behind your desk.

Being switched on means engaging with the wider world.

Leave the office and get out there

You're trying to be switched on. You're trying to find inspiration and empathize with your clients or customers.

Searching for inspiration, you Google "innovative thinking". You get 65 million results. Inputting "creativity" shows 47 million.

You stare at the fern in the corner of your office, willing it to come up with a solution.

Office architecture doesn't conspire to inspire, either with its "greige" walls or its desiccating air conditioning. Not for nothing the downbeat humour of Dilbert, where thinking is discouraged in the cubicles of doom. Rare is the Silicon Valley nirvana of Google's pets at work, fussball tables in the boardroom and rowboats in the brainstorming area.

The simple truth is that your desk is *not* the place to seek inspiration. The only solution is to get out of the office with your recording light on.

What you're lacking is stimulus. The *Switched On* mindset seeks stimulus outside the usual. You need to realize that you're not going to find anything new in the same research report that at least five of your company's closest competitors have already read. Inspiration comes from being exposed to a whole range of new experiences and ideas. And you're not going to find them sitting at your desk.

Free yourself

Before you literally get out of the office, take steps to free yourself from the pointless "busy-ness" of office bureaucracy.

The typical office worker is interrupted every three minutes by a phone call or email or other distraction. The problem is that it takes a further eight uninterrupted minutes to get our brains back into a really productive state.

— Carl Honoré, author of In Praise of Slow

Bureaucracy works against the switched-on mindset. You're so busy with your work schedule in the office, you never have enough time to see what's outside (where your customers and clients are). Everyone is so busy with internal meetings and dealing with the urgent stuff, it is never the "right time" for getting out and getting inspiration. There's never enough time left for the important but non-urgent stuff.

Hierarchy is an organization with its face towards the CEO and its ass to the customer.

— Jack Welch

This comment sums up Jack Welch's no-nonsense view of how he turned GE from a bureaucratic behemoth to a dynamic powerhouse. His solution was to simplify processes and get rid of complex layers of bureaucracy, approvals and formality in order to free managers to be agile, fast and closer to customers, so earning him the nickname "Neutron Jack".

Putting customers first is nonsense unless you've cleaned the crap out to allow people in the front line to do it.

— Tom Peters

I have seen for myself the evolution in culture that happens as a business grows and as a consequence becomes a more bureaucratic animal. And while formal lines of reporting and management systems are crucial when the structure gets bigger, these should not be at the expense of empathy with the customer or of creativity.

We must be wary of becoming too internally focused. There is a very fine balance that needs to be struck between being professional and focusing internally, while still maintaining an external customer-centred focus.

As an individual you can start to reduce the stultifying effects of routine and formal reporting. Look through your work week and see how many of the meetings are only routine and potentially pointless. Cancel those meetings. It is commonly accepted that bureaucracy is bad — so grab that opportunity and reduce the bureaucracy.

If you don't have that sort of free time to dream and muse and mull then you're not being creative.

— Dan Russell, IBM's Almoden Research Centre, San Jose, CA

Back to the floor

Herb Kelleher of Southwest Airlines has a reputation for getting his pilots to staff the check-in desks at the airport. Shut in the tiny cockpit, locked behind a security door with only the occasional contact with flight staff, how are they ever to derive meaning from their job beyond the simple act of getting from A to B?

The same principle goes for sitting behind a screen in an office with several layers of staff hierarchy between you and the customer. This creates a huge disconnect. It is impossible to find inspiration in the real world if you're sitting at your desk.

"Going back to the floor" is another way of putting yourself in the customer's shoes. But it is also a great way of understanding the part you play in the bigger picture, within the company machine, your "cog" in the company wheel. James Dyson gets every employee from the cleaner to the highest executive to try their hand at building a vacuum cleaner on their very first day. It's not only so they can understand the product, but to see how the rest of the company works, what others' experience of Dyson might be. It gives them a fresh perspective on their place within the corporate machine and leaves them open to inspiration when it's called for.

The growing trend of going back to the floor is no management fad. Experiencing what the customer experiences as the recipient, regardless of your position within the corporation, is fundamental to regaining the inspiration and creativity needed to drive the business forward.

Four Seasons, the luxury hotel chain, makes sure all its employees have a first-hand customer experience. All staff, from chambermaids and kitchen staff to the maintenance engineers, are invited to stay in the hotel as a guest. This helps them understand the Four Seasons experience from the customer's point of view.

Looking again at Medtronics, Bill George instituted a Customer Focused Quality initiative to bring all the engineers, scientists and managers into hospitals to witness procedures, just as he had done.

There were a few objections – people claimed they were too busy to sit around operating theatres doing nothing. His answer was how on earth could they design, market and sell pacemakers without seeing the difficulties doctors were having with them?

One sales rep mentioned that a doctor he witnessed doing a pacemaker operation had only done a few implants per year, while he'd done over 3,000.

The sales rep commented to George, "This takes a lot of time, but while I'm with the doctor doing a case, our competitors are on the *outside* looking in."

By going back to the floor you get the inside perspective.

Don't outsource research

If you're looking for inspiration, professional market research reports shouldn't be your be all and end all. Reading facts and figures gathered by a dispassionate researcher doesn't bring the story to life. It doesn't invigorate a switched-on mindset.

I'm not saying that market research reports are superfluous. They are a necessary source of information, especially early on in a project. And they can be helpful when you want to back up your gut feeling with real facts and figures. But you do need to negotiate a fine balance between formal reports and your inner voice.

And never forget that formal reports will most probably be read by your competitors too, so you won't get any new insights. Get out there and do your own research, let your own ears do the listening. There's just no substitute for the motivation and thoroughness you will bring to the job.

A hired researcher will not have the motivation to challenge and absorb information like you will. And they might miss some important signs that you would stumble on if you did the research yourself. You need empathy with your customer to interpret the information you see productively. The good stuff picked up by a dispassionate researcher might get lost in translation.

Besides, while you're doing your research you'll have all sorts of unexpected moments of inspiration. It will make whatever your findings are much truer and more meaningful.

Market research can also be misleading when it comes to new products. We saw in Habit 1 that the market research for Post-it notes concluded that it had no market potential. Arthur Fry was told by the marketing department that customers didn't want his idea. So what did he do? He did his own market research. He left copies of the Post-it note on people's desks within 3M so they could try for themselves. He kept tally of each person's usage compared to tape. And of course they got hooked on them. Gifford Pinchot reports that Fry's conclusion was: "From my own experience of people clawing and scratching to get these things and the use rate they had in comparison to Scotch Cellophane tape, I extrapolated a large market."

If Art Fry had relied on market research results, the Post-it note would never have seen the light of day.

At the other end of the scale, the market research for New Coke was hugely positive. Many taste tests were done and customers loved the sweeter taste. Detailed research concluded that it would be a great success. Yet New Coke was a disaster.

Only a few weeks after its launch, the Coca-Cola HQ in Atlanta received over 400,000 negative letters and phone calls. "Old Coke Drinkers of America" were demonstrating in the streets. Why? Because the research gurus and experts had miscalculated the emotional connection customers had with the old Coke taste.

Steve Jobs, co-founder and CEO of Apple, is quoted in *Fortune* magazine as saying: "We do no market research."

Like Steve Jobs, most entrepreneurs tend not to rely on market research reports for the very simple fact that they can't afford them when they first start. By virtue of necessity, anticipating future needs by being their own customers, rather than relying on focus groups and data, gets entrenched in their psyche. When I started my two businesses, market research was a luxury I couldn't afford, so of course I did it myself. It was basically one huge fact-finding mission.

To research the coffee shop idea, after my "lightbulb" moment I went out in London the very next day, headed straight to a tube station and circumnavigated my way around the Circle Line, getting off at every one of the 27 stops to see for myself what sort of coffee offering was out there. By the end of that day, I didn't just know there was a gap in the market, I'd *seen* the gap in the market.

Even ten years later when I was in a more experienced position and setting up my second company, I still did my own market research for guilt-free sweets. Of course Google made life much easier and the process shorter. But there was absolutely no replacement for going out there and seeing every confectionery or guilt-free product I could get my hands on.

You can't just ask customers what they want and then try to give that to them. By the time you've got it built, they'll want something new.

— Steve Jobs

By not relying only on information being spoonfed to you from reports, you're tapping into your intuition and creating fertile ground for new ideas. Whenever I need inspiration – wherever I am – I feel like I always have a recording light switched on, so even though I may not be actively thinking I will still be passively absorbing a steady diet of information.

Impersonate your customer

You and your customer may be completely different. That is normal. However, it shouldn't stop you attempting to see the world from their perspective, as we saw in Habit 2. Part of that means getting out there and putting yourself in their lifestyle, impersonating them, even for a few hours. Create for yourself a virtual-reality copy of their world.

Perhaps they work on a Saturday and you don't – how different is their commute? Maybe they work shifts – media is very different in the small hours of the morning while you sleep and that influences how they think a great deal. Something as simple as realizing your customer may never have set foot inside a supermarket during normal opening hours can dramatically change your view of their world.

Regardless of the fact that I worked at my business nine to five, I was a customer of the business 24/7. I lived and breathed it. After all, it wasn't much of a chore to sit there and enjoy a coffee!

But not everyone was the same. As the company grew, we began to hire more people, including people who had previously worked for bigger companies. I'd been really excited when we began hiring from these places because I thought we'd get some really great insight and experience. These guys had to be *good* to get where they were.

But I was shocked – even offended! – to discover that the new breed of big-company employees didn't have the same "impersonate the customer" attitude as I did.

I realized this shortly after one of our most senior executives had joined. I noticed him coming to work carrying a coffee from one of our competitors. This happened day after day, in fact week after week, until I finally said something.

We have a policy of checking out the competition (which, by the way, is another great way to get out with your light on, as you will see below), so I remarked that he must have been getting some serious insights to have been spending so long in their stores. He replied no, it was simply the most convenient place to get his morning cappuccino.

Contrary to what I thought, he wasn't impersonating the customer and seeing their experience from their point of view, or evaluating the competition to see how we could improve and stay ahead. He wasn't using a golden opportunity at all. It was just a routine part of his morning commute.

Of course, I'm not suggesting you should be thinking of work all the time. But having your recording light on is a very subtle inner shift. You don't have to be actively thinking to absorb information. You just have to leave the tab running, so to speak, so you're passively absorbing information.

By doing this you put yourself at a competitive advantage within your company and be more inspired in what you do. So use any opportunity you have to experience the business from the other side of the fence.

Royalty only ever smell fresh paint

You want your interactions with customers to be as authentic as possible, so that you get to see the real customer experience, not a stage-managed one.

What tends to happen in organizations with many layers of management is that when you visit, at whatever level you are, a warning goes out from anyone junior to you that the boss is visiting. So everyone puts on their best behaviour. Unfortunately, this gives a distorted view of what the customer experience is really like.

Of course, the concept of mystery shopping isn't new. Most companies employ armies of mystery shoppers to test out their services. But this still isn't seeing the world through your *own* eyes.

Mystery shopper reports are a good check to make sure that what you do already, you're doing right. But you won't get food for thought in a report from a student happy to get a free meal. Get your own first-person account instead.

As I mentioned above, when I was building Coffee Republic I adapted my lifestyle to imitate those of our typical customers. Before we opened our first store, my brother and I would drive every morning to what we thought was the best of the old-style coffee bars. This inspired us to remain excited and gave us continual food for thought.

Once we opened, of course, we had our morning coffee in one of our own bars – a different one each morning and always as a bona fide customer.

Even as the company grew to 15 or so stores and had a head office, we kept that feeling. Meetings were regularly held in bars, and as quality control each employee in the office adopted a "pet" store – a store that was convenient to their commute, so each day they visited their pet store and gave feedback on their experience as a customer. Very often they came back with great new suggestions and improvements.

However, once we grew past a certain size and had to act "big", we lost that culture entirely. It was as if barriers went up around people's desks. I became marketing director and faced corporate constraints and formal lines of reporting. Most mornings were taken up with different forms of management meetings and reviews. This was all happening at head office.

The upshot of this was that the focus moved away from being out there in our bars, where the customers were. There was almost no reason to be out there as it was all happening inside – people to report to, people to please, people to delegate to, people to review.

Instead of each person getting their morning coffee in one of our bars, visits to bars became formal, pre-planned "store visits". But inevitably, on the days of these visits the bars didn't look anything like how the typical customer saw them most days. They were virtually flawless and spotless. We were getting a completely distorted view.

The saying goes that royalty only ever smell fresh paint because whenever they visit somewhere the best foot forward is the order of the day. You couldn't have the queen see your flaws. And that's why pre-arranged visits to your clients or customers are not same as really standing in their shoes.

Become a customer of your competition

Check everyone who's our competitor. Don't look for the bad. Look for the good. If you get one idea, then that's one more than you went into the store with. And we must try to incorporate it into our company.

— Sam Walton, Wal-Mart

Inside your office, you exist in a bubble. Nothing but the company matters. Competitors are represented by numbers and are to be feared when their numbers are good, derided when they are bad.

But outside, in the real world, competitors are just as much a part of your customer's life as you are. So you need to be as intimate with them as your customer is.

You need to know what product or service the competition sells as thoroughly as you know your own company's product or service. By observing your competitors closely (not through market research reports but through real experience), you get amazing insights into what you can do differently or better, or what you do worse and need to improve.

Sam Walton, founder of US retail giant Wal-Mart, became a student of his competitors, spending hours observing their merchandising, especially Kmart which was well ahead at the time. He admits in his book *Made in America* that he even got to visit the HQs of most of the discount retailers.

During my time in the coffee bar world, we always had a joke – which reflected reality – that on each store opening, our first five customers were our five competitors (from the world of coffee and sandwich bars), coming in to check out if we were doing anything new. And similarly, whenever a new sandwich or coffee bar opened we were there on the first day.

When I launched Skinny Candy, it would have been difficult to launch a new range of products without knowing what was there in the market already. Between us, my mother and I must have chewed our way through kilos of sugar trying out different tastes and textures from the competition. How on earth could I know that what we were offering was special if I didn't have intimate knowledge of what else was out there for the dieting sweet eater?

Today, when I'm judging business awards, I always check out what the entrants know about the ins and outs of their competition. That's the only way to appreciate if they're truly switched on to their market.

When you work in a large organization you are more conspicuous to your competition, so you need to find a way to observe them closely and intimately without them catching you out. Going incognito or in disguise, as long as you stay within the bounds of legality, is part and parcel of being innovative.

Open yourself up to the wider world

Some people are great at taking in new experiences. But if that doesn't come naturally, you have to work at consciously injecting fresh experiences into your working life. This could be something as simple as varying your route to work, inviting someone from a different department out to lunch, accepting an invitation you always refuse – anything that shakes things up a bit.

Mentally, opening yourself up is about choosing a different newspaper, browsing sections of book stores you don't normally visit or having a conversation with someone or about something you never knew before. Leaving your comfort zone opens you up to new experiences.

The world's top CEOs and politicians get inspiration from various sources, anything from Chaucer to *The X Factor*.

While it seems simple to pick up *The Guardian* instead of *The Times*, that isn't change. Being different is about challenging preconceptions and dismissing snobbery. It's swapping *The Times* for the *Daily Star*, reading *Grazia* instead of *FT How to Spend It*. The fresh perspective comes from looking in a completely different place, embracing what was once anathema to you.

Management consultant Tom Peters says he routinely picks up as many as 15 magazines from airport newsstands and spends the entire flight tearing out pages from interesting and offbeat articles.

I learn much more window-shopping at Louis Vuitton in Paris than by looking at consumer electronics outlets.

— Ole Bek, quoted in businessweek, 1997

Author, TV producer and journalist Danny Wallace took the idea of turning routine on its head to extremes in 2004 when he wrote *Yes Man*. The book centres around a time in his life when he was stuck in a rut, a slave to routine and blocked to new experiences. One day, he decided to say yes to everything.

That was the best thing in the world. It means you take a chance, grab an opportunity. If you say "yes",

everything can change. If you say "no", nothing ever changes.

> — Danny Wallace: The Yes Man, Belfast Telegraph,
> 13 December 2008

Everything that resulted from him getting out there and just saying yes led to his book becoming a major international film, starring Jim Carrey. Where will exposing yourself to different experiences get you?

Inspiration and creativity will creep up on you

The more you immerse yourself physically in your business, the more inspired moments you'll be exposed to. Out of the chaos you create in your mind, great ideas will simply come to you. By tossing random thoughts into your mind, you create fertile ground on which to cultivate new ideas. Put in the same old, boring information and you can hardly be surprised that this is what you produce.

There is a very simple law in operation here, the first law of creativity – the quality and uniqueness of stimulus in has a direct impact on the quality and uniqueness of ideas out.

> — Sticky Wisdom, ?What If!, 2002

This is a lesson Richard Branson learnt early on. And to make sure inspiration doesn't sneak away again, it has now become a habit of his to carry a little black notebook around, and he encourages everyone else at Virgin to do the same.

Takeaways

Make sure you are bringing a fresh perspective to your working life every day

Never be too busy for creativity

Leave your desk and go for a walk about

Don't let routine dampen your curiosity

Pretend you are a customer of your own company

Pretend you are a customer of your competitor

By wary of formal visits around your business

Deliberately break out of your routine so you can see and think about issues in a different way

Have your recording light on at all times, even when you're not working

Habit 4

The Importance of Being Clueless

Becoming switched on is about forgetting the "this is how we've always done it" mentality and wiping the slate clean
Cluelessness is dumping your baggage and unlearning received wisdom

Henry Ford, America's first car maker, was always trying to make his company conveyor belt go faster. He asked employees with a lifetime's experience how they could do it.

Anecdotally, their response was: "Mr Ford, we have worked on this assembly line for 25 years. Believe us, there is no way it can go any faster."

His response was: "Go find me a 19-year-old who doesn't know it can't go faster."

Ford's determination to find someone untrammelled by experience is the essence of being clueless. Becoming clueless encourages you to dump the baggage that comes with skills and experience and to approach each new challenge with an uncontaminated mind.

Knowledge and experience can put blinkers on your creativity. Becoming clueless removes those blinkers and restores your peripheral vision, opening you up to new ideas and perspectives.

When you don't know what it is you're supposed to see, you notice so much more. That's why great innovations hardly ever come from the establishment:

- Microsoft didn't invent Google.

- Coca-Cola didn't create the smoothie.
- Hoover didn't make the Dyson.

By wiping the slate clean, you open your mind to receive the fresh information that's going to ignite your creative mindset.

Being clueless demands that you subvert "the way it's always been done". As companies grow they acquire a dogma that constrains them. They put experts with experts, marketing with marketing, finance with finance. The first thing that does is shut down individuals' creativity.

Cluelessness gets you out of that stifling situation.

The power of fresh minds

A good way to capitalize on cluelessness is to work with people who are qualified not by years on the job but by attitude towards it – enthusiasm, inspiration and creativity.

Going against the grain of hiring on "skill", not "will", inventor James Dyson is opposed to lengthy CVs, believing that one factor behind his company's innovative products is that it employs graduates straight from university.

The basic reason for this is that they are unsullied. They have not been strapped into a suit and taught to think by a company with nothing on its mind but short-term profit and early retirement.

— James Dyson, Against the Odds, 2003

Similarly, the first Sony Playstation succeeded partly because the young engineers who invented it were new to the video games industry.

We were fortunate because we were amateurs when it came to games and we naively went about doing what we thought would be sure to work. Not preoccupied with established industry practices, we started from square one and let the ideas flow freely without reservation.

— Shigeo Maruyama, vice chairman of Sony Computers Entertainment, quoted in Robert Sutton, Weird Ideas that Work, 2002

You don't have to be fresh out of university with no experience to have new ideas. After all, we can't all stay in that place for ever, and experience can count for a lot. You can still get into the habit of working with a fresh mind.

Perhaps you're part of an established team, each member chosen for a particular skill. This doesn't stop you approaching things in a different way:

- When you're thinking about something, detach yourself from the way it's been done before.

- Don't assume that experts have the answer – what about the ingenués?

Robert Sutton in Weird Ideas That Work talks about Nobel prize winner Richard Feyman who was involved in, among other things, the development of the atomic bomb. He was also the author of a number of books about the joy of thinking for yourself. He refused to read current literature and chided graduate students who began their work in the accepted way, by checking what had already been done. That way, Robert Sutton reports that he told them, they would "give up the chances of finding something original".

Of all the habits in this book, being clueless is the one I hold the closest. I believe that an uncluttered, unfettered mind gives you a huge advantage in seeing things others miss.

In both businesses I've started, my lack of industry experience and knowledge has acted to my advantage. It's given me an open mindedness to just stick to the vision and the end product and make it happen, blissfully unaware of the obstacles on the way. To be honest, I think I've probably had more resistance and discouragement from industry insiders than anyone else.

I remember when I was starting my first business I went to see Russell, a potential supplier. Russell sold coffee machines and my brother and I went to meet him armed with a sum of money from capital we had just raised, ready to pay £5,000 out on a big coffee machine. However, instead of getting us to write the cheque and nailing the sale, all Russell told us was how we shouldn't go into this business, because "his father, grandfather and great-grandfather had been in the coffee business and were adamant that US-style coffee bars would never work".

Today the high street is littered with them.

Avoid the success trap

Steve Jobs, in his now famous commencement address to Stanford in 2005, talks about the days when he was very publicly thrown out of Apple, the company he founded:

The heaviness of being successful was replaced with the lightness of being a beginner again. Less sure about everything, it freed me to enter one of the most creative phases of my life.

This he did by founding movie maker Pixar (of *Toy Story* fame) and computer company NeXt, which was then bought by Apple – and the rest is iHistory!

We all know about the complacency success brings, but perhaps we need to remind ourselves that it has the potential to trap us.

James March, Professor Emeritus in organizational thinking at Stanford University, actually calls this a "success trap" or a "competence trap": your skill set, what you thought was your best asset, becomes a liability. As Robert Sutton remarks in *Weird Ideas that Work*, you become so good at doing something that it prevents you from ever doing anything new.

A good example of the success trap occurred at Xerox. In 1970 developers at its research facility at Palo Alto, California, demonstrated the first ever personal computer. At that point Xerox could have had a five-year head start over its competitors.

But the team at headquarters had grown up and grown rich with Xerox photocopiers and all they saw in the future was selling more photocopiers. So, of course, they didn't want to pursue the new PC. It would almost have been a nuisance for them. Why take a risk on a new product when they already had a cash cow?

The clever engineers who never got the attention of Xerox's top brass ended up defecting to Apple and Microsoft. By the late 1990s Xerox had lost its dominance in photocopiers. Its past success had paralysed it and consigned it to history.

At an individual level, sticking with the status quo even when it's successful eventually switches you off.

The innovation treadmill, where you have to move forward just to stay where you are, is a cliché for a reason: if you're not moving forwards you really are going backwards.

Defeat routine

If you physically follow the same routine – same commute, same desk, same weekly meeting, same report filed on the same day every week – it's difficult to break out mentally.

In fact, if your working day changes little from week to week, year to year, it's hard to see how you can truly engage with what you do. And yet, even the smallest changes can make the biggest impact.

Andy Law, co-founder of St Luke's ad agency, knows that the last thing he wants to do is dampen creativity when it's his business's life blood!

When you come to work in the morning, you never know where you are going to be sitting. There is completely open space here. It's terribly destabilizing not to have your little desk or space where you can put your photograph up. But we decided collectively to do this because we want to defeat habit. Creativity is the defeat of habit by imposing originality and change.

— quoted in Robert Sutton, Weird Ideas that Work, 2002

Another way of breaking out of old habits, if you're really stuck, is to distance yourself physically. A lot of innovations happen in new business units intentionally set up far away from HQ, to get away from the organization's longstanding practices.

At Hewlett-Packard, traditionalists in the company weren't keen on developing printers, so Richard Hackborn, the board director who built HP's goldmine printer business, moved his team as far away from Silicon Valley as he could, to Boise, Idaho. In setting up a separate engineering department far away from HP's core business and the naysayers who told him printers were a waste of time, he was able to create the printers that have been so successful for the company's business today.

In 1964 Lee Iacocca came up with the iconic Mustang, the first inexpensive sports car of its kind, by moving his team to the Fairlane Motel, away from Ford's corporate HQ. He did this because he knew that inside the corporate walls they would be constrained by Ford's past successes and know-how.

So he assembled a mixed-discipline team including design and advertising people, which was unheard of in those days. This team famously became known as the Fairlane Committee, and by only meeting at this motel they were able to bring their idea to life and present management with a fait accompli.

Break the silos – bring in outsiders

Large corporations tend to become compartmentalized – they foster a silo mentality. Marketing deals only with marketing professionals, operations with operations and so everyone gets a narrow view, and no one sees the bigger picture. There is a mentality of doing nothing beyond the job spec.

Another way of becoming clueless and approaching what you do with a fresh mind is to break the silos and find people who don't share the same expertise or experience, so they are not hamstrung by history.

When working with fresh minds you see that you don't have to ask marketing questions of the marketing department. Why not let HR give their view? Get opinions from a mix of teams as often as possible.

But what about taking it one step further? Go outside your business. New research conducted by the Institute for Entrepreneurship and Innovation at Vienna University suggests that there is a lot to be gained from looking outside your business at "analogous" markets, primarily because users in those markets aren't blinded by existing beliefs.

The research brought in three groups of users who faced a common challenge: improving protective equipment. It brought together carpenters looking for ideas for respirator masks, roofers looking for ideas for safety belts and skaters looking for ideas for knee pads. The findings showed that users from analogous markets in general had better ideas than target market users. So for example, the best ideas for improving knee protectors for skaters came from carpenters and roofers, not from skaters themselves.

So it makes a lot of sense to cast a wide net and invite people from analogous markets to your brainstorming. As outsiders, users in similar markets are essentially clueless and don't know how things have always been done in your business, so they can give you many more insights than current users can.

Asking your family (especially kids) for their point of view is also a great way of breaking your habitual thinking patterns. Their perspective, however off the wall, will be great raw material for your new way of thinking.

Don't obsess about competition

There is a great quote I saw once, I don't remember where:

Don't be obsessed by the giant in front of you. Watch out for the maverick behind you.

This is because the maverick is clueless. The problem with large corporations and their competitors is that they subscribe to the same industry magazines, get the same body of research and even hire the same people. The result is that they all follow each other round in a circle and yet somehow expect to have an original thought. It's impossible!

Take Cadbury, which wondered why, with all its years of experience and star employees hired from other great confectionery brands, its own organic fair-trade brand raised barely a yawn from consumers.

It was because while Cadbury and its competitors were watching each other's half-hearted efforts hit the market, a restaurateur and macrobiotic obsessive (about the last person you'd expect to be interested in chocolate) founded an organic food company, Whole Earth, and from there decided he ought to make some high-quality, sustainable chocolate, branded Green & Black's. In 2005, 14 years later, founder Craig Sams sold the brand to Cadbury for a substantial sum.

On an individual level, try to think back to when you were a child, how enthusiastic you were and full of dreams. The baggage may have taken over so you have become heavier and slower in the way you work. You need to return to that childlike state.

Anyone who stops learning is old, whether at 20 or 80. Anyone who keeps learning stays young. The greatest thing in life is to keep your mind young.

— Henry Ford

You become clueless when you open yourself up to start learning again.

Takeaways

Don't be too set in your ways

Work with fresh, uncontaminated minds

- Unlearn how it's always been done

- Don't let your experience or success become your straightjacket

- Avoid the corporate bear hug

- Beware of judging too quickly

- Cluelessness is about leaving the complacency of the comfort zone behind you

- Don't let a "how we've always done it" mentality undermine your new mindset

Not Cluelessness

- This is how we've always done it

- Someone tried it already

- Believe me, I know

- If it ain't broke, don't fix it

- Why reinvent the wheel

- It's impossible

- It's standard practice

Habit 5

Prototyping

Prototyping translates your insights into something tangible
It takes your idea out of the ether and anchors it in reality, helping you and others "get a feel for it"

Can you visualize this product?

- Repositionable
- Handy for ideas
- A work aid
- Bright yellow

If someone asked you to visualize this product, would you have come up with the Post-it note?

Arthur Fry, the Post-it note inventor, had no idea how to put into words the concept of the infamous sticky note, although he knew how they would be used.

His solution was to make samples and pass them around the office for people to try them. And of course, people got hooked on them, as we all have. From those early samples, Post-its now come in 8 sizes, 25 shapes and 65 colours.

Ideas are at their most fragile at the beginning.

A new idea is delicate. It can be killed by a sneer or a yawn: It can be stabbed to death by a joke or worried to death by a frown on the wrong person's brow.

— Charles Browder

Larger organizations are hostile breeding grounds for anything new or different. Prototyping is about doing small experiments at low cost, using what you have to hand. That's why you need prototyping as a useful tool for maintaining momentum and moving ideas forward. It is the art of bringing an idea to life, of making something tangible with limited resources.

It serves two purposes. First, it turns your ideas and vision into something you can touch and feel, and secondly, it helps you make progress by testing for real what works and what doesn't.

Prototyping is not only for inventors. It allows you to see your idea in physical form at the lowest cost, without investing in new systems or buying expensive equipment. Unless you give physicality to that thought in your head, it will just evaporate.

At work we rely on speadsheets, words and memos. In contrast, in real life we often have a more natural, hands-on, "let me show you what I mean" approach.

Prototyping is a way of bringing that palpable approach into your working life.

People "get" prototypes

Rare is the manager who presents a new strategy with a single slide. Rarer still is the manager who produces a prototype of an idea and lets it do the talking for him.

— Jeffrey Pfeffer and Robert Sutton, "The Smart Talk Trap",
Harvard Business Review, 1999

For too long office cultures have relied on memos, reports and slide shows. Long PowerPoint® presentations can often resemble a sketch from *The Office*, with a droning voiceover, endless meaningless charts, and graphics plumbed straight from wordprocessing software.

This kind of approach is disconnected, and the best cure for insomnia known to humanity.

How can an idea grab you as different if it's presented in the same 11 point Arial as every other idea that's come your way? Ideas in written or spoken form, even if they are presented on a chart with loads of really clear diagrams and bullet points, can never be truly engaging or exciting.

Educational psychologist Jerome Bruner of New York University cites studies that show that people only remember 10% of what they hear, 30% of what they read, but about 80% of what they see and do.

Making your idea real by whatever means possible is very important in getting other people to understand it quickly and clearly. By making it real, it ceases to exist only in the imagination and enters an embryonic stage from where it can only grow.

Once an idea is tangible, and people can see it, feel it and interact with it, you have a far better chance of convincing others of its potential.

The old adage that a picture is worth a thousand words is very true for creative thinking. Whereas people might not understand something you are describing to them in words, as soon as you show them a prototype they "get it" instantly.

Prototyping is the best way to move an idea forward and you don't need to be an art graduate or superb engineer to do it. We're not talking about creating architectural models costing thousands of pounds. You don't need a degree in design to create a meaningful model of your idea, as you'll see below.

Anyone can prototype, it's *Blue Peter* stuff

Happily, no special qualifications are required to prototype expertly. We learned the skills watching kids'

TV, doing class projects or whiling away long holidays making scrappy paper boats and planes.

We understood prototyping intuitively, but we've lost this ability gradually as we've matured. And so the task is to bring this childlike curiosity and enthusiasm back into the office. It's a playful, iterative approach that should be part of the workplace.

Prototyping can be doodling, drawing or modelling. It's about creating mock-ups of the end product. Which kind of prototype works best obviously depends on the type of business.

For prototyping, you don't need to invest in fancy new equipment or ask for any permissions. Somehow make do with what you've got. Buying expensive equipment or investing in new systems locks you into one way of doing things and takes away the flexibility you need.

Consumer products can be prototyped from wood, cardboard or foam – anything you have to hand that might make the idea real. But services, internal processes and abstract concepts of all kinds can just as easily be prototyped. For example, role plays bring an idea into a scenario where it is experienced in real life and in real time with human beings, not as written prose.

If it's an internal change you want to bring about, then don't wait until you get a 99% vote from a committee – just try doing it.

By getting hands on and bringing an idea to life, the argument that others find the concept difficult to visualize simply evaporates. Thinking that it's silly to present a model made out of loo rolls to the board isn't thinking creatively.

I always prototype. It's the only way for me to get ideas out from between my ears. I even prototyped this book by sticking each page into a sketchbook so I could visualize it as a book on the shelf rather than a Word document.

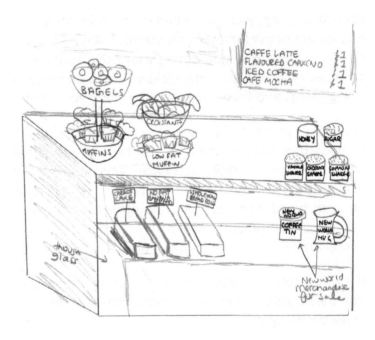

Take a look at my sketch of a visualization of my coffee bar idea straight after I had it in New York. You clearly don't need to be a great artist to get your idea across!

New ideas are fragile – prototyping makes them real

The logic of prototyping is that however good ideas are, they're abstract.

They exist as visions between our earlobes and they are as fragile and fleeting as the bubbles in a sink full of washing-up liquid. They fly in, lit up like a firefly, but if you don't catch them, they burn out.

The best way to snatch that idea – that lucky break – is to make it real. By bringing the idea into the physical world you give it momentum. The only alternative is inertia – and that will kill your firefly stone dead.

In *The Art of Innovation*, Tom Kelley recommends: "There's nothing more powerful than making a few bold lines on a cocktail napkin." For example, CEO Herb Kelleher said that the business plan for Southwest Airlines started with a simple drawing of a triangle. As soon as you start sketching your idea it gets the energy going.

Momentum moves ideas forward

There's no time like the present. As well as enabling other people to visualize your idea, one of the other big advantages of prototyping is that it starts to build momentum.

Grabbing whatever is to hand to express an idea is not elegant or slick, but it is of the moment.

Prototyping is a state of mind. What counts is moving the ball forward, achieving some part of your goal. Not wasting time.

— Tom Kelley

Californian design agency IDEO, of which Tom Kelley is general manager, couldn't wait for winter. It needed to test if its new snowboarding goggles would resist fogging up on the slopes. The issue was that in July its California base obviously lacked snow. Going to somewhere like New Zealand was out of the question. But time was of the essence.

Then the designers had a brainwave. There was an ice-cream factory nearby with industrial-size freezers. IDEO took in a handful of exercise bikes and a wind machine into the factory. With hardy volunteers pedalling furiously to work up a sweat, it was able to prove that its prototype worked, the goggles were fog free.

If your idea is being frustrated because you can't get hold of the right people to speak to, try making them a prototype and leave it for them to digest when they have time. That way, you've taken the first step and got things moving. This also bypasses one of the crucial reasons people respond negatively to new ideas – they don't have the time to get to grips with them.

With a prototype to mull over at their leisure, you give your target time to form opinions, get to know your idea better and let its benefits sink in. Perhaps, in time, you can turn that "no" to a "yes", just as Arthur Fry did when he left Post-it notes on people's desks, a great example of putting prototyping to work.

Anything worth doing is worth doing badly

James Dyson made the first prototype of the bagless cyclone (the first of 5,217, of course) by ripping out the "persistently clogging bag" from a vacuum cleaner and replacing it with a cardboard cylinder stuck together with duct tape.

Even if your first prototype is awful – really embarrassing – it's still a great start. It's really Creativity 101.

Think of it as a stream of creative energy. If you wait too long for the perfect idea, your creativity will stay between your ears in inertia. You find yourself stuck, getting too intense and uptight about it. If you lose momentum, you will falter and eventually give up.

Quick prototyping is about acting before you've got the answers, about taking chances, stumbling a little, but then making it right.

— Tom Kelley

However your prototype turns out, you do get the ball rolling. Even if it's a really, really bad prototype, at least when your colleagues, your boss, even your chairman passes your desk you'll get a reaction. They will comment, you'll get feedback and feedback is food for thought.

[Prototyping is] the equivalent of putting a stick of dynamite down your pants.

— Sticky Wisdom, ?What If!, 2002

When I came up with the idea for Skinny Candy, I had no idea how to start a confectionery company so I went back to prototyping. It was the only thing I knew would get the idea out of my head and into something real.

I ordered loads of confectionery packaging samples into which I decanted normal sweets, playing around with the packaging. After lots of cutting and glueing I ended up with mock-up bags, created in true *Blue Peter* style, which I kept on my desk and in my bag.

The aim was to see and feel something as close as possible to the real thing. This really helped to keep the ball moving.

By having them in front of me every day as actual bags of sweets rather than words in a business plan, I was forced to hone in on the detail. I would show them to other people, and by seeing the bags for real they got a much more accurate feel for what I was planning.

This was a great source of insights and I would take on board all the comments and work them into my next protoype. Bit by bit, very imperfectly, I was fine-tuning the product.

The sellotaped-together mock-up bags of sweets looked like a 5-year-old's art project. But what was important was that they brought the idea to life and gave me and everyone else a better sense of what the product was really like.

Hands-on problem solving

Because prototyping forces you into actually making your idea happen, it also makes you drill down into every detail of what you are doing. And the devil is really in there. It forces you to hone in on all the little things that make a big difference to the end result

We've looked at how standing in customers' shoes enables you to experience what you do from your customer's or client's perspective. In the same way, by prototyping you are making that physical experience real. Doing this helps you to get valuable insights that you can feed back into the next prototype and move closer to perfection. Crucially, prototyping lets you make your mistakes and discoveries as soon as possible in the development process, so you can change things and move on.

This will enable you to present a more in-the-bag proposal when it comes to pitching your idea.

In his new office in Princeton, Einstein asked for a desk, table, chair, pencils, paper and a very large wastebasket: "For all the mistakes I will make."

Prototyping makes you more creative

Prototyping actually goes beyond problem solving. Call it serendipity or even luck, but once you start drawing or making things you open up new possibilities of discovery. You stumble on new ideas when you start doodling, drawing and modelling. It sparks your creative side.

Prototyping gets you in the creative flow – or what athletes call "getting in the zone". So even if you have a kind of writer's block, you still have to go ahead and just do it! Make something. Even if it's awful, it will get your creative juices flowing.

If all else fails prototype till you're silly.

— Tom Kelley

When you prototype it takes you into the customer's shoes. You are feeling and experiencing what the customer would experience. It immediately gives you a new perspective and sparks your muse.

Prototyping forces you to examine what your idea is really about – things you may not have imagined before.

And the great thing about prototyping is that it activates your right-brain thinking. It removes some of the automatism of office routine. You're doing stuff that's real, using 100% of yourself. Prototyping is using skills for DIY, bringing hands-on playfulness back into the office – and a bit of playfulness is what we need to invent the future.

Takeaways

Prototyping makes your idea tangible

Just start – wherever, whatever – get going

Prototyping helps you and others get a feel for your idea

Playfulness activates your right-side, creative brain

Start sketching your ideas

Space mind-expanding mock-ups around you

Prototypes help you experiment under the radar – use whatever you have to hand

Anything worth doing is worth doing badly!

Habit 6

Notching Up Nos

Stepping outside your comfort zone and challenging the status quo is bound to meet with resistance because there is a bias towards the status quo

To be switched on you need to change your attitude to "no"

We are regaled by success stories every day. But here's what they don't reveal:

- Howard Schulz approached 242 people to raise money for Starbucks and was rejected by 217 of them.

- Walt Disney was turned down for a loan for Disney theme parks 300 times.

- Colonel Sanders went to 1,000 restaurants before someone bought his KFC chicken recipe.

- Paul McCartney failed his audition for Liverpool Cathedral Choir.

- Elvis Presley got fired after his first performance.

I believe one of the biggest obstacles to *Switched On* thinking is our attitude to rejections and failures.

We need to accept that any move away from accepted norms, trying out new and different ways of doing things and not doing what we have done every day, we will inevitably make a few mistakes, fail a few times and hear the word "no" quite often.

Yet companies don't factor this in. There seems to be a particular stigma attached to hearing "no" in a corporate situation.

As an employee, you hope the words "Yes! You're hired" are the first in a long line of yeses. It's easy to fall into thinking that it will be plain sailing from there on.

After all, you have joined a successful company. It is big and well established, so what it is doing must be right and there is no need to push too hard as it is already successful.

Without realizing it, you get into the mode of thinking that you have "arrived" and that there will be no need to change the way anything is done. The clients are there and money is coming in. In fact, on the surface it seems that taking any kind of risk or making any change is completely unnecessary, and would even be foolish.

Even if you were able to set aside this natural acceptance that it is unnecessary to challenge the conventional ways of the company, and you did consider suggesting alternative ways of approaching things, there remains an even bigger incentive not to push too hard: the threat of corporate Siberia.

Being on the receiving end of a "no" carries a lot of stigma. A "no" makes you feel like you are bad at your job, that you have made the wrong decision. You become concerned that if you notch up any more "nos" the pink slip indicating the sack will soon be winging its way to your in-tray.

The corporate environment isn't only uncomfortable with the idea of notching up "nos", it often appears openly hostile to it. Mistakes are not to be supported, much less encouraged, and the corporate message tends to encourage people to play it safe and minimize risk at any cost.

And yet you are expected to be innovative.

It is wishful thinking to expect change without factoring in a few failures along the way. The paradox is that companies are so keen for employees to embrace change and adapt, yet they put a high price on failure and getting a "no", and mistakes are not easily tolerated.

Making change happen is messy and formal organizational structures need to get used to that.

If I had to do it all over again, I would have encouraged employees to make more mistakes.

— Thomas Watson, IBM

One of the most important habits of being switched on is not to avoid nos but actively to seek them. I call this notching up nos. They are an inevitable part of having a switched-on mindset and moving out of your comfort zone.

The founder of Honda once famously said: "Success represents 1% of your work that results from the 99% that is called failure."

I believe in this so strongly that if I'm not getting nos in my own life, I immediately start to worry that I may be too deep in my comfort zone, just coasting along.

In 1995, trying to get a £90,000 loan for our new business idea, my brother approached about 40 bank managers. From these initial approaches we got 19 face-to-face interviews.

These 19 interviews resulted in 19 rejections. All the bank managers we saw came back with the same response: we are a nation famous for tea drinking – coffee bars will never take off!

We could easily have stopped there. After all, 19 nos is pretty unanimous. But we knew that a concept that was catching on like wildfire in America would also work in the UK. We loved it ourselves as customers. We knew there was a gap in the market.

So we persisted – and the twentieth bank manager said yes.

This story is in my first book, *Anyone Can Do It*. I approached writing that book in much the same way: I had a list of UK business publishers pinned to my wall and sent them all a proposal for my book. As their replies came in I crossed off the ones that rejected it.

But the more names I crossed off, the closer I knew I was getting to the one who would publish my book. And eventually one publisher, the right one as it turns out, said yes.

I do accept that it is easier to have this cavalier attitude when you are working on your own. You are able to keep a low profile, it is only you who hears the "no", and you never need to see the person who rejects you ever again! But I believe this attitude should be fostered in large companies as well.

I realize it seems counter-intuitive, but you do need to stick to your guns, and you just have to notch up enough nos until you finally get the yes. There are no short cuts.

In fact, if I get a yes too quickly I'm almost alarmed that something is not quite right.

It may seem ridiculous, but the number of nos you can expect is almost directly proportionate to how prolific and creative you are being.

The American poet WH Auden put it well: "The chances are that, in the course of his lifetime, the major poet will write more bad poems than the minor." Why? "Because major poets write a lot."

This observation holds even more true in the world of work. If you're not getting nos you're not trying. I got my yes at number 20 and founded Coffee Republic; these were a lot fewer nos than Howard Schultz of Starbucks. Go figure!

> **We should do something when people think it's crazy, if people say it's good it means someone is doing it already.**
>
> — Hajime Mitari, president of Canon

No one is born persistent – it's not genetic!

When we look at the number of rejections and obstacles other people have overcome to achieve something great, the first thing that comes to our mind is: "That's not me. I don't have the persistence gene." We immediately label them as persistent, courageous types.

There's no such thing. No one is born with unbreakable tenacity. It's not a mysterious formula that some of us can generate and others can't. It's there, it's simply dormant.

If it was easy everyone would be doing it – it's the hard that makes it so great.

— Anon

Think of persistence as a muscle you haven't exercised for some time. The corporate environment and the prevailing attitude that you don't need to, or shouldn't, push too hard have let your persistence muscles atrophy.

Switched-on thinking gets them moving again. And as you flex your muscles, you make them stronger.

Notching up nos isn't magically going to take away the unpleasantness of rejection. You'll still want to go and kick the chair or find that you boil with frustration. But when you know it's part of the switched-on process, it becomes so much easier to keep going.

When the world says, "Give up," hope whispers, "Try it one more time."

— Anon

The shock of the new

In its default setting, the human brain prefers the familiar. It tends to follow the same well-trodden paths.

Take supermarket shopping as an example. Behavioural studies have shown that for a significant period of time, shoppers are on auto-pilot, or "grab and go". It doesn't matter what you do to price or packaging, when it comes to essentials in particular, shoppers will automatically buy the same thing each time.

So when we are faced with a new idea – in the shopper's case, say a new brand of cereal or washing powder – our brain wants to reject it. Humans are hard-wired to resist new, unfamiliar, challenging behaviour.

In business it's no different. "A definition of a lousy product is one that has no enemies within the company" says Jack Welch. Old ways are preferred over new ones, new versions of old projects a safer way to "innovate" than breaking out of the paradigm and starting over.

Einstein called innovation "an act of creative destruction" and of course everyone resists destruction.

If you truly understand that innovation is an act of creative destruction, you can understand why you meet resistance whether your idea is ground-breaking and transformative or is only a small change to how you normally do things. However amazing your idea, by doing things differently you don't have be a nice niche to fall into.

When you hear about people spotting a gap in the market, that makes it sound pretty easy. But so-called gaps in the market are always hypothetical. They are not like empty seats on a plane you can slot yourself into. Every gap is created by destroying an element of the old way of doing things. And by their very nature, people who are used to the old way of doing things will resist it and you. So you have to squeeze and push into the gap, against great resistance.

With every new idea I've started I've factored in the liability of newness. The journey of turning the idea into a reality meant I had to navigate an obstacle course of rejections and nos. In fact, any new creative endeavour, from making a movie to starting a business to launching a new way of doing things in a large company, is an obstacle course.

For my first coffee bar idea, first I had to get past the bank managers. Then it was suppliers. Even though we were paying them, they still didn't want to supply us with products, as we were an unknown commodity with an unproven track record.

And then it was customers. Sometimes the biggest resistance to innovation comes from the people who will benefit from it most. Customers can be very conservative, very unimaginative. Very unimpressed with the idea that you are so taken with.

With my first business, it took my brother and me six months to turn customers round and convert them to the US-style coffee bar idea. Those six months as we dejectedly watched customers walking past, frustrated because we knew we had so much to offer, were the most demoralizing months of my professional career.

In those first months our customer base was mainly our mum coming in and drinking as many cappuccinos as humanly possible. But we stuck at it.

We knew deep in our hearts that the customers would come round eventually. Because we were our own customers, we knew. We simply focused on converting one customer at a time. Unlike us, they hadn't spent the last 120 days living, eating, breathing, sleeping what we were offering. They'd had barely a minute as they passed the store. With enough persistence and time, they'd come round eventually! Thankfully they did and our first bar reached breakeven.

So factor in that by changing to a switched-on mindset and initiating new ideas, you will face the liability of newness. You will meet resistance just because your idea is new.

It's not failure, it's trial and error

When trying out new things, you're bound to fail at some stage. Apple's Steve Wosniak views failure as a thinking strategy: "Every failure is a learning experience and it should be seen as part of the process rather than the enemy."

Instead of thinking of failure as a final result, think of it as part of the creation process. Take it as constructive criticism.

James Dyson didn't invent the iconic cyclonic vacuum cleaner by happy accident:

I made 5,127 prototypes of my vacuum before I got it right. There were 5,126 failures. But I learned from each one. That's how I came up with a solution.

— James Dyson, quoted in "Failure Doesn't Suck", Fast Company, 1 May 2007

It was Dyson who rejected his own models, but the idea is the same. He endured 5,126 failures before he got it right. In his case, failure was an editing process.

It was the same with Thomas Edison, who said:

> **I didn't fail 700 times, I just found 700 ways that don't work. I have succeeded in proving that those 700 ways will not work. When I have eliminated the way that will not work I will find the way that will.**
>
> — Edison

If you're trying something new or different, you're going to make a lot of mistakes. Trial and error are inevitable.

Mistakes are part and parcel of good business

The thinking goes that the price of making mistakes is too high to pay in business. There is a fear of sticking out, of rocking the boat.

But you mustn't let this stop you. As we have already seen, in truly innovative – and successful – companies mistakes are encouraged, not punished.

GE bought Kidder Peabody for $600m. The acquisition was a disaster and led to heavy losses – but no one got fired. New Coke was a cataclysmic disaster for Coca-Cola – but no one got fired.

In the words of Don Keough, Coca-Cola's chairman: "These failures are just a price of staying in business."

And according to Jack Welch: "I've rewarded failures by giving out awards to people when they've failed, because they took a swing."

It's the same at Southwest Airlines. Someone decided to start a cargo business on the side, with the aim of competing with FedEx – it was fiasco, yet still no one got fired.

Similarly, I'm sure that for every iPhone and iPod that Apple comes up with there are many new products that don't see the light of day. Still the room to make mistakes is there and that's why Apple can come up with so many market-busting innovations. The same culture that spawns those innovations inevitably produces some duds as well.

The opposite of success isn't failure, it's doing nothing.

Where you stumble, your treasure lies.

— Joseph Campbell

Fear of failure holds you back as an individual. It pins you down in your comfort zone. Getting beyond that is truly being alive and switched on in what you do.

> We admire instant brilliance, effortless brilliance. I think quite the reverse. You should admire the person who perseveres and slogs through and gets there in the end.

> — James Dyson, quoted in "Failure Doesn't Suck", Fast Company, 1 May 2007

Takeaways

- Expect to hear a lot of "no"s when you are out of your comfort zone

- Beware the status quo bias

- Anything new or different is met with resistance

- Remember, the only way to avoid a "no" is not to try

- A "no" is just someone's opinion

- Persistence is not a personality trait, it's a skill you can develop and practise

Habit 7

Bootstrapping

Bootstrapping is the art of execution and getting things done with limited resources. It recognises that you can't execute new ideas down conventional channels.

Become a doer and not just a thinker

Aparticularly common trap in business is to think you've got some great ideas, you're empathizing with your customers, you've got energy, you've got a good strategy to take your ideas forward, and so you believe the rest will take care of itself – the company machinery will transform your vision into reality.

It won't.

Ideas are easy. It's the execution that's hard.

— Jeff Bezos, founder of Amazon

Implementation is much much more important than strategy. Without it you are no further forward than before you had the idea.

I used to think small companies were great at ideas but bad at implementation, and that big companies were bad at ideas but great at implementation.

How wrong I was. It is in fact the reverse. Small businesses are much better at implementation. With fewer people, fewer systems, less bureaucracy, everyone gets stuck in and makes things happen. But as these companies grow, so does the bureaucracy.

There are so many chains of command to get past, so many different departments to go through, so many rules and processes that ideas don't become reality. They get stuck in bottlenecks. They get stuck at implementation.

The frustrations that someone with a switched-on mindset will face in a large company structure are a bit like sitting in a traffic jam, waiting for every red light at every new junction. It saps your energy. It's the corporate traffic jam that delays and eventually stalls new initiatives.

In contrast, bootstrapping takes you on a different route so you circumvent the energy-sapping traffic jam altogether.

The expression "by hook or by crook" may seem a bit careless in a formal corporate environment, but it's important. It's about getting things done no matter what. It may be a really imperfect way of getting it done. But don't worry, you can tweak and upgrade how you get it done later. The key is getting over the initial hurdle of making it happen. That is what this chapter is about.

What is bootstrapping?

Dictionaries variously define bootstrapping as "using one's own initiative" or "carried out with minimum resources or advantages".

Bootstrapping is most commonly associated with the kitchen table business start-up, the lone entrepreneur –

not with the culture of big companies. Examples such as the King of Shaves founder Will King personally filling 10,000 bottles of shaving lotion, The Body Shop founder Anita Roddick selling shampoo at her first shop in Brighton, and the image of Bill Gates and Paul Allen pulling all-nighters programming for Microsoft spring to mind.

Yet a bootstrapping culture is something that is absolutely essential in a large organization if you want to be able to generate new ideas and new ways of doing things and actually make them happen.

It is about not necessarily always going down conventional channels or going by the book. Instead, you just get on with things.

Bootstrapping helps you go under the radar and avoid what Gifford Pinchot in *Intrapreneuring* calls the "corporate immune response".

You need to "Just Do It"

In the creative world, ideas are worthless unless they are acted on. It's not enough to invent something brilliant – the world is full of unfulfilled inventors. James Dyson would be just another dreamer if he had not acted on his great idea of the dual cyclone.

OK, it may have taken him from 1983 when he developed the technology to 1993 when he sold the first one in the

UK and turned it into the world's fastest-selling vacuum cleaner. But he did it. He executed his brilliant idea, and that's what counts.

In large companies, too much emphasis is on so-called high-level strategy and not enough on implementation. People often gripe that ideas hang about too long, going nowhere. This creates a stifling situation, long on frustration and short on energy and fulfilment.

Execution is mistakenly thought of as merely something routine and easy that simply gets done. It is something leaders often delegate while they focus on issues they perceive to be bigger.

But execution is not routine. It's actually very challenging. It has to be built into a company's strategy, its goals and its culture.

How you execute a strategy is even more important than the strategy itself. And everyone, from the leader down, has to be deeply engaged in it and make every effort to make it happen. If they don't, it simply won't happen.

Execution is not a job too big or too little for anyone.

In *The New York Times* bestseller *Execution: The Discipline of Getting Things Done*, Larry Bossidy and Ram Charan claim that lack of execution is: "The single biggest obstacle to success and the cause of most disappointments."

There no such thing as a genius idea. Ideas are a dime a dozen. Hundreds of people had seen US coffee bars and some may even have thought about bringing the concept to the UK. In fact, ideas like that are somehow in the ether – lots of people can catch them simultaneously. But my brother and I rolled up our sleeves and actually did it. That's the big difference.

It's the same with business plans. Anyone can write a great business plan, full of great ideas and big dreams. But a successful business on paper doesn't translate into a successful business in the real world.

A business plan is a worthless piece of paper without someone rolling their sleeves up, getting their hands dirty and turning it into a living, breathing, operating business.

Simon Woodroffe, who started the YO! Sushi brand, tells a great story of being the first person to come up with the sushi bar conveyor belt. While developing the concept, he was told that in Japan they also had robot drinks trolleys. He realized this would be a great gimmick, but simply had no idea how or where to get hold of a robot. In true bootstrapping style, he did some research and was given a telephone number to call at Edinburgh University. According to Simon:

Guess what? The phone rang and was answered with the immortal words, "Robot Department, how can I help you?" Three hours later I was speaking to Martin who had developed a system for robotic wheelchairs and was willing to help me.

— Simon Woodroffe, The Book of Yo!, 2000

The result is that today customers are urged out of the way in YO! Sushi restaurants by particularly tetchy automated drinks trolleys. That's the power of bootstrapping.

Woodroffe would never have got his iconic drinks trolley by waiting for typical drinks equipment suppliers to start manufacturing them. He bootstrapped and got it done. You have to just do it to make things happen.

Sneak under the corporate radar

It's easier to get forgiveness than permission. If you wait for permissions and authorizations, your ideas will stall and never see the light of day.

Arthur Fry did quite a bit of work on his Post-it notes in the corporate shadows before he stuck his head above the parapet. In his initial stages of execution he couldn't make them into pads that stacked on top of each other. So he kept his less successful versions a secret. He burnt all but his most perfect examples to keep the idea of failure away from the corporate doubting Thomases. By the time 3M management saw the concept, it had been executed so well that it was practically a fait accompli.

All the innovators I've talked to who work within large companies say they tend to do quite a bit of guerrilla work to make things happen. They try to do things on a scale small enough so they don't need to get authorizations and avoid the tracking system that might stall their initiative.

Bootstrapping bucks convention

You can't always execute new ideas through conventional channels. The book in "going by the book" won't have instruction for anything new – it will only have instructions for the old ways of doing things. Using old channels to implement new ideas can be much like banging the proverbial square peg into a round hole.

By moving away from conventional channels I'm not suggesting you reinvent the wheel. But instead of sticking to the same company processes you will find yourself crossing silos and breaking down the artificial barriers between departments. Returning to Arthur Fry again: he was a chemist, but that didn't stop him turning into an engineer when the occasion demanded it.

Equally, looking for answers and resources in the same old places is fated to bring the same old results.

My brother and I experienced this when we were opening our first coffee bar. We wanted to hire a new breed of "baristas" to bring true New York-style coffee to the UK. We were very aware of the importance of providing superior, enthusiastic and different customer service from the outset. These were the people who would introduce the UK to tall half-caff skinny vanilla lattes. They had to be mould breakers.

I remember we put our advert in the London *Evening Standard* on a Tuesday, because we were told that this was what everyone in catering does. The next day we were inundated with over 100 phone calls from prospective employees – people who had worked in the sort of establishments that provided the mediocre customer service we wanted to distinguish ourselves from.

We were attracting exactly the calibre of staff that represented what we didn't want to be. But what should we have expected? We were going down the same old routes we had been fighting so hard to distance ourselves from.

The only standard of customer service we really admired was a new sandwich bar chain. Their employees were highly trained, buzzy and very enthusiastic – just what we were looking for. But we couldn't afford to train them up ourselves, even if we'd known how. So we bootstrapped.

We figured that if we poached two of their employees they would come ready trained. And they could teach us all about customer service and how to train. We printed out little strips with our name and number and headed off to one of their bigger shops.

After much embarrassment and shifting around we attracted the attention of Max and Miguel, who accepted our offer of 50p extra per hour. It was only once they actually joined us and before opening that we realized there was one small hitch. They didn't speak English! Doing the best I could, I spent the last two days before opening giving them an – extremely! – accelerated English course that consisted mainly of explaining that it was rude to say "what?" to customers. It was by no means perfect, but mastering the subtleties of Shakespearean English could come later. They had the right attitude and we could open the store – that's what mattered.

We had realized that going down the conventional route of hiring people wasn't going to give us what we needed, so we went for the unconventional. It wasn't perfect, but it got the job done.

I used some unconventional routes to get my confectionery idea off the ground as well. Rather than trying to research the nutritional content of a gram of chocolate, I found myself using my kitchen scales to weigh sweets whose packets already gave me the calorie count per bag, and working it out that way.

I'm sure the big confectionery conglomerates have teams in white coats performing experiments with pipettes to gauge the precise carb/calorie proportions down to the last nanogram. My way was unconventional, but it got the job done.

Bootstrapping is not beautiful

"Anything worth doing is worth doing badly" is a motto we've seen before. In the prototyping habit, where we first learned this, we saw how to make an idea real. Bootstrapping is about actually making that idea happen, but the same rule still applies.

By bootstrapping you get things going, however imperfectly. There will be plenty of time later to improve how you do things. The stickler is getting it going the first time.

3M's Arthur Fry wanted a way of getting his new sticky pads produced. But the way the company was organized, designing the production of Post-it notes was not Fry's job. He was supposed to design and the engineers were supposed to make the products.

Of course, manufacturing told him it was impossible to make his invention using 3M's existing technologies. But Fry was having none of it, so he invented a machine himself.

Again, the engineers said his creation would be impossible as it would be hugely expensive and take six months to build. He wouldn't accept that either so he built a crude version – overnight – and it worked! He cobbled together in one night what, if done the conventional way, would have taken six months. It wasn't perfect, but it got the job done.

When building my confectionery business I remember the first order I got from Harvey Nichols – it was for 4,000 bags to be delivered on 1 December. What the department store didn't know was that I was packing them all from home in a spare bedroom – just me, my mother and my PA. We were printing the labels on an £80 inkjet printer, measuring each bag on the kitchen scales (we eventually upgraded to Food Standards scales), heat-sealing them and living with a spare room full of wholesale boxes.

I panicked so much once the order from Harvey Nichols arrived that I ordered three pallets of wholesale sweets to be delivered to my flat. What I hadn't factored in was what three pallets looked like (clue: it's an *awful* lot) and how much space they'd take up! And where was my flat? Up three flights of stairs with no lift.

Seeing that carrying three pallets of sweets up three flights of stairs was an impossible task for my mother and me, I went round the corner to a building site. I offered £20 each if some builders would haul the sweets up the stairs! Several brickies later and working round the clock to pack all 4,000 bags, we got them in on time.

Had I waited to do this all perfectly – scouted a storage unit and packing area, chased packaging suppliers instead of Harvey Nichols buyers – I would never had got sales going. Of course, once I was off and running I was able to upgrade this procedure, have the sweets packed in pre-printed bags in a factory, stored in a storage depot and delivered in vans – not the back of my car!

The devil is in the detail

I don't want to over-generalize, but there is a tendency as a company gets larger to leave the details to routine. An important part of the bootstrapping culture is realizing that execution is not about getting the big things right. You have to pay attention to the little things as well.

And it doesn't matter how high up or junior you are – you still need to focus on the detail. I read an article recently about the UK CEO of IKEA. He was nonchalantly telling the story of when the founder Ingvar Kamprad came to visit. On the morning of his visit they went at 5 a.m. to the Croydon loading bay and talked to the drivers. I was surprised that the billionaire – and somewhat aged – founder would even bother with the loading bays at 5 a.m., still less go on to spend the rest of the day on the shop floor. This is obviously indicative of someone who really understands the adage that it's all in the detail.

An almost obsessive attention to detail is in fact a trait all great business leaders share. Sam Walton chose every one of his first 130 stores. Until Wal-Mart grew to 500 stores, he continued to keep up with every real estate deal the company made.

While heading up Microsoft, Bill Gates reportedly reviewed all the code his programmers wrote. It's all in the detail no matter if you are a multibillion-dollar powerhouse or just an employee with a good idea!

Michael Dell says he learned this lesson from his computer company's weekly customer meetings:

We began to realize that customers were less focused on what the industry calls "big things" – such as product features or hot technology – probably because those needs have largely been satisfied. We were fascinated to learn how the "little things" became "big things" to the people who really mattered.

This goes against the instinctive thinking that big business heads don't really bother with little details, that they focus on the big picture and leave the detail to others. In fact, they focus meticulously on the little things. This is a lesson for everyone at every level.

That's why execution is not routine. It's about all the detail you need to focus on. And that's why bootstrapping is something that cannot be delegated. The focus on detail gives you the momentum to drive through the corporate traffic jam, the bite-size approach makes it easy to tackle any problem, and the understanding of minutiae provides credibility and support for your case.

As the saying goes, you can eat an elephant if you break it into small chunks.

Would you trust someone else to take responsibility for the details of your idea? If you did, you'd be putting the crucial task – that of making it happen – into someone else's hands. Bootstrapping isn't necessarily about physically taking charge of everything, but you must be hyper-aware of all the constituent parts.

I strongly believe in the importance of every little detail. Take branding as an example. No matter how trivial the process seemed, I've known that brands I've built were the sum total of every single step. A million and one details together formed the message we were trying to convey. We would argue over whether a cake plate was "us" or "not us". The ingredient label on the back of a packet of Skinny Candy represents what the brand is about. Ingredients are not a detail the technical factory churns out. It may seem obsessive, but considering the different ways you can name something as basic as "gelatine" is often what will make the biggest difference to your product.

Even the font of the "best before date" matters. The people behind Innocent smoothies invented the concept of "enjoy by" rather than "best before by". There's something in that. Innovative crisp makers have stamps like "fried by Kevin", "fried by Ian". There's something in that too.

To give an example that sticks in my mind, we searched high and low for a "push/pull" sign for our door. We couldn't afford to do a branded one, but we didn't want a stock brass sign because those are so redolent of the old-style sandwich bars that we wanted to supplant. It seems a tiny detail, but the message it gave out was huge.

Momentum

A big benefit of bootstrapping is about doing things *now* and not waiting for the "right time".

Somehow there never is a right time for trying out new things. You just have to make the leap and do it. It gives you the power of momentum to your idea and momentum is what you need to keep going.

Amazon.com's founder Jeff Bezos is a great example. In Spring 1994 he got into his car and was typing out his business plan as his wife drove round the US looking for a base for operations. Seeing the internet grow at 2,300 per cent in April alone, he knew he had to move fast. He also had to move "cheap", having already thrown in his job.

With these twin imperatives snapping at his heels, he pulled together a website that was basic but worked, and settled in Seattle, a town already brimming with the resources he would need.

His bootstrapping created the features that ensured Amazon is now one of the most successful online retailers. The site works quickly, serves the customer well and sticks to what it's good at: selling products and delivery efficiently.

Bezos's "time is precious" logic gave him such a head start on the web that bricks-and-mortar bookshops didn't have a chance of catching up.

Money is a poor substitute for creativity

If I'd had shed loads of money I'd have done everything wrong.

To an extent entrepreneurship is survival and that survival mode is what nurtures creative thinking.

— Anita Roddick, The Body Shop

The reason for the energy in a newly started business is that the lack of resources forces people to think in a more creative way.

As companies get bigger and more successful, resources become a cushion and you're no longer forced to think creatively. Instead you go by the book, fall into a rut and coast along.

Bootstrapping imposes the discipline of not merely throwing money at a problem. And this is a very good habit for every individual in every company to get into.

Bootstrapping forces you to use your imagination a bit more. It requires you to plumb your full range of resources and squeeze every drop from them.

Certainly it helps when times are tight – when you're asked to make 2 + 2 = 5. But you're only using half your potential if you stop there. Bootstrapping is using the company's resources in the most productive way and your individual focus becomes laser sharp.

Look at Jet Blue, an innovative American low-cost airline. It wanted its call centres to be based in the US rather than outsourced to some operator thousands of miles away. And it obviously wanted to make money in the process. What was its boostrapping solution? It invented homesourcing – its agents are mostly stay-at-home mothers picking up calls from their homes. This negates the cost of a call centre, yet means the customer gets the satisfaction of always speaking to someone in their own country.

The lesson: you don't need to throw money at a problem – just a bit of blue-sky thinking!

And bootstrapping is also a kind of insurance. It guarantees your ownership of the project. Because the discipline of bootstrapping has made you drill down into the detail, made you think about every angle and exploit every resource to make it happen, no one can claim credit for it but you.

Takeaways

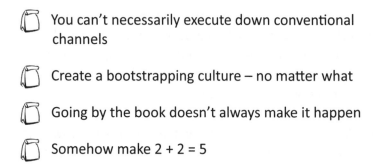

You can't necessarily execute down conventional channels

Create a bootstrapping culture – no matter what

Going by the book doesn't always make it happen

Somehow make 2 + 2 = 5

Don't worry, you can improve and tweak it later

Go under the corporate radar.

It's easier to ask for forgiveness than permission

Lack of money makes you more creative

Bootstrapping gives you momentum

Habit 8

Taking 100% of Yourself to Work

You bring more than just your CV to work.
Being switched on isn't just about 100% effort,
but also 100% personality.
In tapping the full potential of your creative
mindset, you need to use 100% of yourself

This is the last chapter on being switched on, but it's actually what this book is all about. It's about leaving behind the traditional thinking that work is work, play is play and never the twain shall meet.

That's out of date. Obsolete.

Life is no longer a series of compartments into which you slot depending on the time of day. Switched-on thinking is about realizing that what you do at work bleeds into every area of your life and vice versa. And realizing that this is not a negative thing.

What it all boils down to is being 100% yourself.

Being in so-called work mode isn't a case of putting on a suit and leaving your non-work personality behind. It's about making an emotional connection with what you do – and you can't do this if you're suppressing most of your emotional self in a bid to be more "professional".

Being switched on is about bringing your head and your heart to work. This requires us to dispel some myths.

Myth 1: The work–life balance

In the 1950s, the concept of work–life balance meant dad would arrive home from work to find mum happily home-making and the kids would be presented for half an hour, scrubbed and ready for bed.

Moving on to the 1980s, Gordon Gekko ruled the boardroom, greed was good, lunch was for wimps. Since then we've moved into a touchyfeely era when it was decided that family was as important as work and should be made time for – as indeed it should.

But that was when you could leave work back at the office. Largely due to developments in technology and changes in expectations as a result, that argument has become obsolete.

The boundaries between work and life have broken down. You get a work email sitting on a chairlift 3,000 feet up on your skiing holiday. Your pocket vibrates just as you're sitting down to Sunday lunch with your great-aunt. You surf the net in your downtime at home, but you still check your work email every five minutes. You even check your work email before you leave … for work!

If we want people to do only company work while they're in the office, shouldn't we also have corporate police to make sure they're not working on company business on weekends?

— Ricardo Semler, The Seven Day Weekend, 2003

There is no getting away from work – technology has made it so. Work–life balance has become a foolish term, because the lines between "home" and "office" are completely blurred.

For those who fought so hard for the fabled work–life balance in the first place, this may seem like a huge slip back into the dark ages. But the intrusion of technology doesn't mean you have to have a 24-hour slog, day in and day out.

There is a quid pro quo. The same way work seeps into your personal life, your personal life should be able to seep into your work too. The coat over the chair idea of nine to five presenteeism should have gone out with the ark.

Companies are realizing that in order to retain talent, they need to allow the flexibility to work smarter. This isn't some fringe idea that is yet to go mainstream. In 2006, *The Economist* noted:

For some time to come, talented people in the West will demand more from employers and clever employers will create new gewgaws to entice them to join ... for a growing number of these workers the most appealing gewgaw of all is the freedom to work as and when they please.

— 'Life Beyond Pay', The Economist, June 17 2006

Myth 2: All work and no play

Those of us in the developed world spend around three-fifths of our lives working, with the other two-fifths taken up with childhood, retirement and sleep. Is it fair that we should spend such a large chunk of our lives doing something that is the opposite of play?

Work is an integral part of life, not a weighty counterbalance to it. There is something very wrong with the picture of hating what you do, dreaming of weekends and wishing your life away towards retirement.

In fact, the opposite of work isn't play – it's idleness. That's why men who work all their lives die soon after retirement. Several studies have found that people – and men are in the majority here – who do not find stimulating activities following retirement, die or develop serious illness within a year or two of finishing work.

You need to make work a fulfilling, enjoyable part of your life because it's simply a waste of your life otherwise. And there's a direct correlation between how much you enjoy something and how well you do it.

Myth 3: They're not paying you to enjoy yourself

This is what I used to hear as I went about my first job as a solicitor in a London law firm, asking why we weren't having fun.

It's a complete myth that business is not meant be fun and that good business is serious. By fun I don't mean wearing party hats or having conga-line Fridays. Nor is it about enforced fun, where every employee is pressed into an activity that is inevitably described as "wacky", "crazee" or some other misnomer. Nor is fun about being in a constant state of fevered excitement.

Fun at work is about the satisfaction of doing really well and performing at a high personal level. The phrase "time flies when you're having fun" sums up the joy of being engaged in what you do – what athletes call being in the zone.

In essence, becoming switched on is a wake-up call to catalyse your energy, attention, passion and creativity.

There's too much sobriety in the workplace. It's too dry, too shut off from the rest of the world. You need to bring more fun into your life at work. That element of play and originality releases your right-brain creativity.

> **Fun is not a form of entertainment, it's an integral part of being good at what you do at work.**
>
> — Daniel H. Pink, Free Agent Nation, 2002

Jeff Bezos tells a great story in a clip on YouTube about the early days of Amazon. Staff programmed a bell that would ring every time they got an order, so the whole office could celebrate and feel the excitement. In his own words:

> *There was great moment when we were examining every order that would come into Amazon and it was always a family member placing the order. The first order we got from a stranger, a dozen or so of us gathered round asking: It's not my mom – is it your mom?*

After the first 30 days the bell rang so much it got annoying, so they turned it off.

Myth 4: Be "passionate" about your job

Yes, you read that right. I was surprised myself that I put this as a myth. On the face of it, it goes against everything this book is about. But what I mean is that the word "passion" is becoming overused and it puts everyone under pressure to find it.

You end up questioning what you do because this elusive "passion" doesn't seem to exist for you. You compare yourself with others and feel you fall short.

Don't sit there night after night questioning why you can't fall in love with this widget you produce. It's understandable that a washing machine sprocket is hard to love. The idea of passion sets up an expectation that cannot be met.

Instead, think of passion as doing something to the best of your ability, so that you're in the zone. Passion in this sense is about using all of who you are.

Rather than constantly talking about "passion", serving customers passionately, filling in blue forms passionately – organizations should make employees feel exhilaration once in a while, let them get involved to a point that they shout "yes" and give each other high fives because they did it their way – and it worked.

— Ricardo Semler, The Seven Day Weekend, 2003

You can't fabricate passion. If you don't find it, you can't go for motivational training and hype yourself up. You can't find passion if you are not being yourself in your life at work and unleashing your whole being. You can find passion by following the habits in this book and emotionally connecting with what you do.

finding 100%

Here are a few different ways of putting your whole self into your work.

Find the click

Were you excited and apprehensive when you went for the job interview? How did you feel waiting for the job offer letter? And how did you feel once you got it?

The sense of potential, excitement, opportunity ... ?

That gut feeling that kept you up late and got you up early is the spark you need to reignite your enthusiasm for the job. There must have been something about the job that appealed to you, something that clicked with you and attracted you to that particular field or profession as a means of earning a pay cheque.

You need to retrieve the same emotional connection that sent you to work with a spring in your step and butterflies in your stomach that very first day.

Ekhart Tolle in *A New Earth* talks about the enormous empowerment of having enthusiasm for what you do:

Unlike stress, enthusiasm has a high energy frequency and so resonates with the creative power of the universe. Sustained enthusiasm brings into existence a wave of creative energy, and all you have to do is "ride the wave".

— Ekhart Tolle

Use your reservoir of talent

Everyone has a wealth of instincts, interests and skills that combine to form their talents. Some refer to it as a "calling". Whatever its name this reservoir can be deeper and more diverse than even the holder himself realizes. The best way to ensure job satisfaction in the long run is to exhaust that reservoir. After all, no one works for money alone.

— Ricardo Semler, The Seven Day Weekend, 2003

By a certain stage in life, we all know who we really are, what we like, what we are good at, what we are weak at, what we hate doing and, most importantly, what we love doing.

By definition, your talents are going to be found in the things you love doing. It doesn't take a genius to realize that you tend to be good at what you love doing!

Even if someone only wants a simple nine to five job, aiming to make enough money to meet their needs, they ideally want to be happy while doing it. To achieve that, they still need to tap their reservoir of talent.

Basically, the attitude of "it's not my job" and merely working within your remit doesn't tap your reservoir. You need to push beyond that to feel exhilaration in your working life. It's the accountant who doesn't just fill in a tax return, but finds new opportunities for your business to grow. It's going the extra mile.

This is why it is so important to take 100% of yourself to work. Maybe 60% is required for you to do your job, and that other 40% – that's what's needed to *love* it!

Align your personality with your work

This is a twist on the previous point. It should be pretty obvious to most that if you're a people person you will not be happy or do well in a job that is just desk based, with only yourself for company!

When you feel you're an outgoing person yet your job relies primarily on quietness and discretion, you will naturally feel as though you're walking on eggshells. At some point your personality will win through and force you into a situation that is at best inappropriate and at worst leads you to make mistakes. The stress of trying to prevent that is unnecessary and counterproductive.

Equally, a quiet, measured person will feel over-whelmed in a scenario that requires continuous networking, relentless socializing. This will bring feelings of inadequacy that lead the person and inevitably their bosses to believe they are not doing their job properly.

Aligning your personality with your job removes that stress, because you are not constantly trying to police yourself as well as do what is needed.

Yet it's surprising how far our career progression and success lead us away from where we started and the area we excelled in. Promotion is great, but how do you reconcile the desire for promotion and progression with the need to continue working in a way that suits your personality? We often feel that we have to change the way we behave when we change jobs or move up the career ladder.

Being switched on doesn't mean changing jobs or refusing promotion. It means having an open and honest dialogue with your bosses and colleagues. Are there elements of your job to which you are eminently suited and others to which you are not? Find ways around the latter. Can you delegate, share tasks, refocus until you are using the very best elements of your personality to their greatest effect? And this isn't negative for your boss either. They want to make sure

that they are making the very best of their resources –
including you.

Your self-interest and the company's are the same

Aiming to stave off boredom during the corporate day is
not counter to your bosses' ambitions. Your happiness
and engagement – protecting your self-interest – will,
in the long run, be in the corporate self-interest too.

Coming into work on autopilot doesn't do you any
favours. You can't possibly be doing a good job if you
are switched off and disinterested, turning up and
doing just enough to get by. Actors call this "phoning it
in". That's simply not good enough any more.

A word about diversity

As a female in business I always get asked about diversity,
especially the issue of gender diversity. For me, the
essence of diversity is being 100% yourself. For women,
instead of emulating men, it's about acknowledging
the differences. Men and women are different and
each gender can own up to those differences. We work
differently. We think differently. We have different
aspirations. We define power and success differently.

So the real challenge today is for women to find a way
to combine their personal priorities with their work

priorities. Simple gender identity doesn't come into it. The challenge is to find a new way of working that complements our lives rather than compromises them, striking a balance between how we would like to live our lives and how we would like to work.

Diversity has nothing to do with colour, race, gender or disability. The essence of diversity is acknowledging that individuals are just that – individual. It's the same if you're a single white male, you still don't want to be subject to a cookie-cutter vision. You want to be an individual. Forcing uniformity doesn't foster productivity; quite the reverse.

100% me

On a personal level, I bought into the importance of being 100% myself because I started in a career that didn't suit my personality. It didn't play to my strengths, namely optimism and enthusiasm.

I'm a people person who essentially landed herself a desk job with little or no contact with the outside world. My solution at the time was simply to leave, but at that point I hadn't realized how I could have stayed, by changing my mindset and finding a part of the job that was in fact aligned with my personality.

Had I not tapped into my reservoir of talent, I would never have understood that I had this creativity inside me. Instead, I'd have plodded along being mediocre and largely unfulfilled.

In my case, my brother Bobby switched on the light for me. He made me appreciate that there was something that needed my people skills, my tenacity and my "have a go" mentality.

I realized that there were many similarities between the switched-on entrepreneur and the switched-on employee. Since then I've obviously gone on to other things. There's Skinny Candy, which satisfies my still twitching entrepreneurial side, but there's also my work with companies from which this book was born.

You can find again the buzz you felt when you walked through the doors on that first day.

You can break out of autopilot and feel alive in what you do.

You can be 100% yourself and completely, fully *Switched On*.

Takeaways

 Re-evaluate your frames of reference about your life at work

You don't need to leave your emotional baggage and personality at the door

Work and play should not be opposite words

There is a direct correlation between how much you enjoy your work and how well you do it

Switched On is about bringing all of your self – your head, heart and personality – to work

Afterword

I am well aware that there is a certain irony to me writing this book – effectively an entrepreneur writing an ode to corporate life. It's true that I probably am best known for starting my own businesses. But outside of those two businesses, I have worked in and worked with large organizations throughout my career, and through this mix of business experiences it has become strikingly clear to me that there are strong parallels between the way an entrepreneur tackles their work and the potential there is for an employee to do the same.

There's been a glut of books singing the praises of the lone-wolf entrepreneur. Entrepreneurs have been put on a pedestal as an example of all that is great about business, at the expense of the employee. I felt it was time redress the balance.

Before writing this book, I started giving talks to companies about how much I wanted employees to begin feeling this buzz that I had found in my work. I wanted them not to see how it was completely possible use all the entrepreneurial habits not to merely survive at work, but thrive – to get to a place where coming to work is much, much more than a means to a pay cheque.

So instead of being odd that an entrepreneur such as I would write a book for people working in big companies, it's actually the most natural thing in the world. I want to give you these steps, these habits, these tools which will hand you back the joy of work.

Because let's face it, working for a big company you have all the benefits at your fingertips. You have company resources to "play" with, you have colleagues to bounce ideas off and become inspired by, you have permission to stretch your boundaries yet the comfort of a regular salary, and you have a holiday allowance to cushion you. The comfy bit of the comfort zone isn't all bad!

Jack Welch had a great vision when he called for everyone to see within a big organization a band of small businesses. They would take the strength of a large company, yet act with the agility of a small one. He talks about using the corporate umbrella to protect you. Instead of letting its size paralyse you, let it liberate you.

In the style of Rudyard Kipling's famous poem "If", if you can use everything about being an employee that's great and that's good, let it liberate you and move you to better things ... then the earth is yours and all that's in it.

The choice is yours. The future clearly belongs to the switched-on employee. And I hope this book provides you with the tools and inspiration you need to change your habits. I want you to be able to capitalize on the freedom, excitement and success that your organization affords you. Go for it now and live the life you were meant to be living.

You wander from room to room

hunting for the diamond necklace

that is already around your neck.

— Rumi, 13th-century poet

Becoming Switched On

Believe Anyone Can Do It

The question is not "Do I have it in me?" but "How do I switch it on?"

Use the skills of everyday life in your life at work.

Put Yourself in Your Customers' Shoes

Make an emotional connection with your customer. Putting the customer (and not your boss) at the centre of your world will give you more meaningful motivation than just coming in for the pay cheque.

Get Out of the Office

Creativity is borne of inspiration and perspiration – neither of which you'll find sitting behind your desk. Engage with the wider world. Leave the office and get out there.

Become Clueless

Becoming switched on is about forgetting the "this is how we've always done it" mentality and wiping the slate clean. It means dumping your baggage and unlearn received wisdom.

Prototype

Translate your insights into something tangible. Take your idea out of the ether and anchor it in reality. This will helping you and others "get a feel for it".

Notch Up Nos

Step outside your comfort zone and challenge the status quo. This is bound to meet with resistance, but to be switched on you need to change your attitude to "no".

Bootstrap

Bootstrapping is the art of execution and getting things done with limited resources. It recognizes that you can't execute new ideas down conventional channels. Become a doer and not just a thinker.

Take 100% of Yourself to Work

You bring more than just your CV to work. Being switched on isn't just about 100% effort, but also 100% personality. In tapping the full potential of your creative mindset, you need to use 100% of yourself.

Sahar Hashemi's Story

Sahar Hashemi is the creator of two brands, earning her the title of "pioneer to the life of the nation" from Her Majesty The Queen. She has been named one of the most influential women in Britain by the *Daily Mail*, was a Young Global Leader at the World Economic Forum in Davos and was one of *Management Today*'s top 35 Women in Business under 35.

Sahar's first business success was Coffee Republic, the UK's first coffee bar chain, which she founded with her brother Bobby in 1995. She grew the business to 100 stores and a turnover of £30m before exiting in 2001. She then went on to found Skinny

Candy, a guilt-free confectionery brand, which she sold to Glisten plc in 2008. Sahar is the author of *Anyone Can Do It: Building Coffee Republic from our Kitchen Table*, which became a bestseller and has been translated into six languages.

Following the success of *Anyone Can Do It*, Sahar has been a much sought-after keynote speaker on the innovation mindset. In the words of one testimonial, "Her passion for innovation energizes the room – she is the verbal equivalent of a double espresso." Companies found that the message from the book, initially aimed at entrepreneurs, was just as appropriate for people working in large businesses.

It hit the right note at the right time, as corporations saw the need to move away from formal, structured and therefore staid organizational behaviour towards a more nimble-footed, agile approach, in what was becoming a continually changing business arena. The recurring brief for Sahar's speeches was to get the point across that it was no longer enough simply to turn up and do your job; a level of engagement and emotional involvement by the employee was required. It was this that had many parallels to the entrepreneur's world. The "entrepreneurial mindset" was becoming a buzzword for employers.

Sahar told her audiences the story of her personal entrepreneurial journey, how an idea came into being at her own kitchen table, and uses the power of storytelling to bring to life the new mindset that people want to ignite. She showed how the basic ingredients for the journey of the entrepreneur are the same as that of a switched-on, awake, engaged and fully involved person working for any company. That the excitement of meeting new challenges at work every day is not the sole preserve of the entrepreneur; that the employee is empowered to control their own career trajectory as much as the entrepreneur. The companies Sahar addressed wanted her to explain to their teams that this enthusiasm and engagement were there, just waiting to be exploited.

The response to Sahar's speeches time and again was that people wish there could be some kind of "takeaway" that employees could use to reinvigorate the enthusiasm she had awoken in them in the conference hall. And so *Switched On* was born.

All the advice in *Switched On* is eminently actionable, by anyone, in any organization.

Early days

Sahar is fond of saying that if you ever want proof that an entrepreneurial mindset is not genetic, you just need to look at her. She didn't come from a family of entrepreneurs. There was none of this "making your first million in the school playground, dropping out of school and hawking products from a suitcase" that is so much a part of entrepreneurial lore.

Instead, she followed the path of education according to convention and indicated no creative traits or business flair in childhood. Quite the reverse of unleashing their creativity and trying out childhood entrepreneurial ventures, Sahar and her brother were taught to study "useful" subjects and aim for solid professions. So she went on to read law at Bristol University.

However, Sahar believes that the most important lesson she took from her upbringing and one that has stood her in great stead throughout her life is the value of discipline and hard work. What you put into something determines what you get out. She's very keen on the maxim "Perspiration, not inspiration" and this carries through her work and her speeches today. Essentially, if you get stuck in and stick at it, you can achieve anything.

On graduating, Sahar trained and qualified as a solicitor with prestigious law firm Frere Cholmeley in Lincoln's Inn Fields. This was a realization of her childhood dream and the culmination of hard work and many hours of exams. It is testament to Sahar's determination that she should achieve this, because it took her four attempts to secure the place. Competition was fierce, and unsurprisingly so. The lawyer's life at Frere Cholmeley was dynamic and everything Sahar hoped it would be.

Nevertheless, while she initially found life as a trainee enthralling and learnt a lot, she started to wonder whether her finely planned choice of career was right for her. This became a bigger doubt for her once she qualified as a solicitor. She found too much of a disconnect between her personality and what was required of a solicitor. In her role she was required to be marked, measured and prudent, whereas she wanted to make things happen. She was a people person who had landed herself a paper-based desk job.

She began to realize for the first time that although she was going to work every day, she was only operating at 60% and was leaving the rest of her personality at the door. She felt it was such a waste to be in a job where she was not able to be 100% herself. She understood how important it was to align her personality and her work. Furthermore, it was clear to her that her lack of fulfilment was actually making her mediocre at her job.

Today she reflects that the lure of the comfort zone made any inclination to change her circumstances impossible, so she was simply plodding along. Without a catalyst, we all find it difficult to change.

For Sahar, the catalyst for change, as so often, came from adversity. In January 1993 her father died suddenly from a stroke. This shock was a wake-up call for Sahar in two ways. It was a reminder that life is both finite and short. But more than that, coming from a very close-knit family, it shattered her comfort zone. This family tragedy highlighted that this comfort zone was in fact a mere illusion, a false sense of security. This was a paradigm shift and helped her to make the drastic changes she knew she had to make. This meant leaving the law.

The light bulb

Sahar decided to leave London and took a trip to visit her brother Bobby, who was living in New York and working as an investment banker. An early riser with jet lag, Sahar stumbled on a coffee bar called New World Coffee on Madison and 44th Street. It was there that she experienced for the first time a specialty coffee bar with its skinny lattes (a real novelty at the time), fat-free muffins and everything else that made the experience seem like a haven of luxury in the hustle and bustle of the day.

On a reciprocal visit from her brother after she returned to London, Sahar raved about how totally in love she was with these incredible New York coffee bars, how much she missed them already and how much she wished they had the same thing in London.

Of course, she was speaking as a consumer only. But as she was enthusing on the subject, somewhere in the back of his mind Bobby remembered that an ex-colleague had put the prospectus of a budding US coffee chain on his desk some time ago. The chain was called Starbucks and it had brought to his attention the enormous coffee-drinking boom that was occurring in the US.

So Bobby had the light-bulb idea. He determined there and then that he and Sahar should start up a chain of US-style coffee bars in London. His three words were: "Let's do it."

Sahar's immediate reaction was firm resistance. She protested vehemently about any involvement on her part. She recalls what she said: "You got me wrong. I meant why doesn't someone else open US-style coffee bars? I will happily be their regular customer. I only liked the coffee bars as a customer."

However, Bobby managed to persuade her by offering to pay her to do the research on his idea for one week only, and then he said it would be her decision whether to move the idea ahead or not. Weighing up the thought of another demoralizing week of not working against the prospect of earning some cash, Sahar reluctantly agreed to Bobby's proposal.

So the next morning she walked to her local Tube station, bought a one-day travel pass, and circumnavigated the Circle Line around London, getting off at each of the 27 stops. She went around a two-block radius of each Tube station to inspect what was on offer to the commuter in search of a cup of coffee.

She loved what she saw. There was obviously a huge demand for coffee, though the product itself was horrible. Queues at sandwich bars for coffee, queues at fast-food outlets for coffee, queues at kiosks for coffee. But Sahar could see that the product being served was essentially brown sludge in a grubby polystyrene cup covered by an ill-fitting lid (which, thankfully, is now a distant memory for most of us).

Sahar remembered from her lawyer days how important the morning cappuccino was. It occurred to her that the reason the coffee was so poor was because all the outlets she visited were essentially focused on other products. The sandwich bars were really in the business of making egg mayo rolls and coffee was very much a sideline. Nevertheless, it was obvious that coffee was being sold in huge volumes.

So the light bulb also turned on for Sahar. She had seen the gap in the market for herself. London was missing out on the New York-style coffee experience. Sahar had fully bought into her brother's idea. She was in, and that was the minute Coffee Republic was born.

FACSIMILE: 10:00PM, 5 NOVEMBER 1994

Bobby,

I CANNOT believe what I saw today on my Circle Line trip. I had honestly forgotten since my lawyer days how totally grim the take-away offer is. London SO desperately needs NY style espresso bars!!

This is how I've summed up the status quo:

• You leave the tube station on your way to the office. Being the London we know and love, it's a cold, grey morning. You're chilled to the bone and half asleep. You can barely face the day ahead. You need that cup of coffee.

• No choice, so you invariably enter a basic, undecorated, local sandwich bar. This is nirvana if your idea of calm and relaxation combines a healthy dose of formica, a lot of linoleum, some residual grease stains, and a smattering of grime.

• You stand in a long queues and watch staff go about their work. That's making sandwiches, by the way!

• While queuing you stare at an exhibit that even an avant-garde modern artist couldn't come up with. Rows and rows of plastic tubs filled with congealed crab mayo, congealed tuna mayo, congealed egg mayo and ashen slices of what once passed (a long, long time ago) for roast beef, the sort which had seen better days in the eighties. None of the above have even been turned over from the day before to hide the glutinous crusts that have formed on their surfaces. Not a nice sight at 8.00 a.m.

• The sandwich maker who is taking your money with his bare hands (note hygiene, or the lack of it!) makes you a quick cappuccino on the side. You can't decide whether you're more worried that he hasn't washed his hands because he might have been to the bathroom, or because he's touched the food that I've described above! You think you could catch something either way!

• You get your hot drink (which I am loath to call coffee) in a polystyrene cup that goes floppy in your hand. As for the lid, well, it's a flat plastic thing with a nasty little hole in it that fits about as well as shoes that are two sizes too small, meaning that if you want to walk with your coffee, burned hands are part of the experience.

- In short, morning coffee in London is not a great deal of fun, unless you like feeling hassled, grubby and unmotivated. By the time you get to work, you hate the day already.

This is what our new style coffee bar will provide:

- You leave same stifling tube station.

- But you enter a place distinctly designed and branded to enhance your coffee experience – a comfortable, warm environment able to accommodate a big volume of traffic yet to be inviting and accommodating at the same time.

- Although you are queuing you can listen to gentle, soothing music and view the delicious range of tempting coffee compliments while you do so.

- You are served by uniformed, highly trained 'baristas' who make your coffee to order and to your individual requirements with four types of milk, strength, decaf, half-caf, iced, etc.

- You take away your coffee in a specially designed and branded sturdy cup with a domed lid which doesn't steal foam off your cappuccino. Plus, you have four choices of toppings to round things off.

Who wouldn't go for it? Surely everyone would love it? In the US they've taken a basic commodity and made it into pure luxury – but not any luxury – a luxury that's part of your daily commute. Happiness, in other words, at the most stressful time of the day.
Thinking of possible strap lines:
It's a break from the daily grind.
It's like upgrading your day!
It's an affordable luxury.
Treat yourself.

It's all so exciting: It feels so right!

Sahar

The rest is the stuff of coffee-bar legend. They both left their respective flats and moved home with their mum to immerse themselves in a world they knew nothing about.

Making it work

In Sahar's words, she was "clueless" about coffee, retail and branding. All her friends were lawyers and all Bobby's were bankers. They gave themselves two months to immerse themselves in everything there was to know about coffee and coffee bars and retail in general. Of course they couldn't afford formal market research, so they undertook a fact-finding mission themselves, with the aim to become world experts as quickly as possible.

They read about coffee wherever they could, drank it as much as possible, visited as many suppliers as would see them, went to any free training courses, visited other retailers and new food concepts. They would spend days on the phone trying to get random information from suppliers – who would often slam the phone down – but one in ten might want to chat and tell them the business inside gossip they needed to know.

Sahar found that their cluelessness actually gave them an advantage. They weren't contaminated by how things were done or by established industry practices. All they saw was their vision of what they would like to experience as customers themselves.

Their solution to branding was simple. They knew they wouldn't be there to tell the customer everything the company stood for, so they made sure the brand did the job for them. They made it speak on their behalf to the outside world. Coffee Republic went on to be named by the *Financial Times* as one of the brands representing New Britain, along with Orange and Carphone Warehouse.

Sahar and Bobby then set about writing a business plan, originally under the name Java Express as they didn't yet have a name for the business. But as we see in Sahar's rule "Anything worth doing is worth doing badly", if they had waited to write the perfect business plan the idea would never have seen the light of day.

According to their business plan, they needed £90,000 to open the first bar. So they started calling random high-street banks. They notched up 19 rejections from bank managers who told them coffee would never work in a nation famous for tea drinking. But they persevered because of their guts and faith in their idea, and eventually the 20th bank manager agreed to give them the loan.

However, they needed to draw on their creativity even further when they almost lost this deal because they were not able to provide security. Sahar searched around the problem, convinced there must be a way, and finally came across the Department of Trade and Industry's Small Firms Loan Guarantee Scheme. This was a little known government scheme at the time (although now very widely used) whereby the government would guarantee the bank loan, and Sahar and Bobby were among the first entrepreneurs to use it. This attitude to thinking around a problem enabled them to make progress with their idea.

Nevertheless, their fight wasn't over yet. It was the implementation stage that really proved their entrepreneurial mettle. Ideas are a dime a dozen, but Sahar proves that it is the execution that really counts. Finding premises, suppliers and employees was all harder than they thought. They discovered that suppliers didn't want to deal with them, even though they had the money in the bank. Landlords didn't want to lease them premises. They were an unknown commodity, no one knew what these new-style coffee bars were – this was what Sahar often refers to as the "liability of newness".

When they did find suppliers who would take their money, they couldn't because these companies weren't making the equipment that made the coffee Sahar wanted to make, and the machines didn't fit the US-style cups that would define the new bars. Sahar and Bobby were swimming against the tide. It soon became very obvious to them that they were introducing a fresh mindset to the market and current suppliers were closed to any possibility of changing their well-established systems.

Time and again they found themselves resorting to bootstrapping, consistently coming up with creative solutions to fill in the gaps between what they wanted and what was out there. Some solutions were less ideal than others – they resorted to FedExing US-style coffee cups across from the States (very expensive and impractical) – but always found a way to get the job done and achieve the next step.

And so the first Coffee Republic store opened on November 3, 1995 on London's prestigious South

Molton Street. Although it was the first coffee bar of its kind to open, and there now seems to be one on every corner, it was by no means an overnight success. For days, even weeks, the new business made around £200 a day, sometimes not even that. But through the persistence of focusing on every little detail and "converting one customer at a time", the tide eventually turned in their favour. After six months sales began to rise very slowly, and momentum started to build as loyalty to the concept and brand recognition gathered pace – people began getting used to walking into work with tall skinny vanilla mochas.

Building a chain had always been part of their plan from the outset. The initial coffee bar was never supposed to be a one-off outlet. Once the first bar had found its feet, Sahar and Bobby opened 2 bars the following year, and then escalated this growth each year to 7, then 30, then 60, then 80 and by 2001 they had 110 company-owned bars. Coffee Republic was named by Deloitte Touche as the second fastest-growing company in the UK.

With growth came the inevitable change in culture. The company moved from being a rather chaotic entrepreneurial one, living on its creativity and alternative thinking, to a bigger, more formal organization with a structure. Much-needed systems began to be introduced, with accompanying controls and checks. They upgraded suppliers to the bigger, more professional ones and strengthened the team, as they were now attracting great CVs. These were all positive developments, but the downside to them was the resulting shift in the company's culture. By virtue of its success, it moved away from its initial clueless thinking and bootstrapping, and the creative "can do" energy of the early days began to be stifled.

Finding it difficult to strike the very fine balance between entrepreneurial and professional approaches to business, Sahar left Coffee Republic in 2001 and sold her shares. At the time of her leaving the company had a turnover of £30 million and 110 stores. Today Sahar openly says that she counts leaving Coffee Republic as one of the greatest mistakes of her life. She was subscribing to the old-school thinking that the entrepreneurial phase was over, and abiding by the unspoken rule that it was time for the founders to depart as the passion and creativity of the early years was no longer needed, to be replaced by systems and management skills.

Anyone can do it

It was only after she left Coffee Republic that Sahar realized that her dream, the idea of working doing something she loved every day, had become a reality in her journey to build the company. It hadn't felt like work. This is what she had been looking for when she left the law firm.

To fill the void, Sahar immersed herself in a new project, and within three months had started writing a book about her experience. She never had a dream of writing a book, but it turned out to be a cathartic experience to go back over the events that had unfolded since death of her father. It was through writing this book that she realized the distinct steps along the path to entrepreneurship, and in fact any creative process that takes an idea from a very fragile bubble in the head and turns it into reality. It became clear to Sahar that anyone can learn the behaviours if they follow the steps. If she could do it then "anyone can do it".

Anyone Can Do It went on to become a bestselling book. Sahar and Bobby were the first entrepreneurs to record the ups and downs of their business journey for all to read and even today the book has a strong following among aspiring entrepreneurs. In a Shell LiveWIRE survey of inspirational role models, Sahar was named 5th, only coming after the likes of James Dyson and the late Anita Roddick.

Skinny lattes to candy

It was while promoting her first book, as she travelled across the UK and internationally, that Sahar stumbled on her next business idea. She has a sweet tooth but decided to give up sugar and sweets on a health kick, only to realize that life's actually rather bland when you deprive yourself of sweets. So she would search out low-calorie sweets on her travels and always carry a stash with her.

Echoing her first "light-bulb moment", the second was her mother's casual observation over dinner one day that if she couldn't find them in the UK, why didn't she start a business making them? There must be a gap for them. This time Sahar's reaction to the idea of starting a business and pursuing an idea was obviously very different: she now knew that being a customer would actually put her at an advantage. Inspired again by a concept she had seen in the US, Dylan's Candy, the energy was there to start a low-calorie confectionery brand aimed at women who, like her, love sweets and chocolates and yet are stereotypically filled with guilt.

So Sahar started at the kitchen table again, believing this is the only way you get an idea off the ground quickly. She went right back to basics and followed the steps she set out in her first book. She did the research herself, but admits this time Google made the process much faster. Her research involved buying every kind of low-calorie diet confectionery she could get her hands on. Then by looking through ingredient labels and tracing manufacturers back through the internet, she was soon able to get her head around the main manufacturers and suppliers of diet sweets.

She came up with the "aha" name of Skinny Candy for her new business. This was neatly reminiscent of her credentials of being the first to bring skinny lattes to the UK. She hired professional designers to design the branding and, roping her mother in, she set about prototyping the sweets.

The home printer ran hot as Sahar mocked up bags of sweets, then carried them around with her all day to see if the packaging was strong enough, light enough and easy enough to compete with other brands already out there. The prototypes slowly evolved into the real thing, still all done at home but using fully hygienic equipment. Soon she was buying bulk confectionery from suppliers and packaging them at home with ingredient labels printed on an £80 printer.

Sahar happily admits that this time she pulled a couple of strings to get her sweets stocked. Her obvious first choice was Coffee Republic. Initially, the confectionary appeared in three Coffee Republic stores on a trial basis (they would only accept a trial), but this gave her a good chance to test out her packaging. Sahar and her mother would deliver the stock themselves to each store.

Then Sahar was given a golden opportunity to get Skinny Candy into Harvey Nichols in time for the Christmas sweet rush, when figure-conscious women were no doubt looking for a festive alternative to the mountains of chocolate on offer at that time of year. It was an opportunity not to be missed and Sahar jumped at it. But that's not to say it didn't cause a logistical headache. They were still packing and labelling the sweets from home – in pure bootstrapping style she had even learned the art of barcoding on a home printer.

The sweets were a great hit with London's fashionistas, who craved the sugar hit without the attendant increase in waistline. As orders came in from Selfridges, Topshop, Holland & Barrett, Whole Foods and finally Waitrose, Sahar was able to upgrade her production systems, in small incremental steps: at first she was buying bulk from wholesalers and packing the sweets at home, then she bought in bulk from factories, still packaging them at home, and eventually she got factories to package the confectionery. By this time it was quite a relief to have distributors and proper storage rather than keeping everything in her spare room!

Sahar admits that the advantage she had this time around was in the PR she received – she managed to publicise the brand name by getting the product into all the high-fashion goodie bags. Skinny Candy was named "hip confectionery brand" by *Vogue*, was on the *Vanity Fair* A-list and was hailed by glossy magazines from *Tatler* to *Grazia*.

In 2007, two years after she started Skinny Candy, an email pinged into Sahar's inbox from the CEO of a big confectionery company which had noticed the brand. This is the sort of email entrepreneurs dream of, their little brand being noticed by a bigger player. After much discussion about visions for the growth of the brand, Sahar received an offer to buy the brand from Glisten plc, a growing confectionery company. With her regrets about leaving Coffee Republic fresh in her mind, this was not a straightforward decision for Sahar. But she could see that this was a great opportunity to take advantage of the distribution channels and know-how of a large, established corporation. It had the capacity to take Skinny Candy to the mass market and also to make the products in its factories across the UK. Sahar liked the entrepreneurial style of the CEO and the creative approach of the team members and so eventually decided to sell half the company.

Switched-on mindset

As we have seen, Sahar Hashemi is guided by what she is passionate about. And as she has shown, following your passion is not necessarily an easy road to take. It's fraught with breakthroughs and breakdowns, ups as well as downs, euphoric highs and heart-breaking lows. She admits that giving life to a new business, which is a living and breathing being in her eyes, is not simple. And she has found it difficult to cut the umbilical cord as she has watched from afar the businesses she nurtured into life, especially Coffee Republic, go through difficulties.

But for her there is no other choice than following what you love doing. Sahar is out to prove that the fulfilment and engagement in work that have traditionally been the sole domain of the free-range entrepreneur are there for the taking for everyone. *Switched On* describes her belief that anyone in any job should always be themselves. That leaving a part of yourself at home is a poor use of anyone's resources. And that by being flexible and tuned into your needs and those of your company, you can be far more effective in your work and get much, much more out of it personally.

Having seen the transformational effect possible in big companies that have actively asked their employees to pitch new approaches and systems and that have encouraged innovation, Sahar believes that there is much to be gained from leaving behind complacency and changing mindsets. For her, the next "gap in the market" for all companies should be to focus on the untapped potential within the business. Therein lies the next big thing.

References

McGee, Paul (2006) *S.U.M.O. (Shut Up, Move On): The Straight-Talking Guide to Creating and Enjoying a Brilliant Life*, Capstone.

Murray, W H (1951) *The Scottish Himalayan Expedition*, J M Dent.

Time (2007) "The brain: How the brain rewires itself", *Time*, Jan. 19.

References

Acknowledgements

When I work on a book, I tend to bite off than I can chew. I have ideas all buzzing around in my head but an inability to articulate them on paper.

When it comes to writing I have a rather unpleasant combination of ideas streaming through my head at 110mph coupled with a writing ability of, at best, 1 mile an hour. That's why I am especially indebted to those without whose patience, guidance and help this book would still be just an idea.

Holly Bennion, my editor at Capstone, who from the beginning shared my vision for this book, and showed admirable persistence in convincing me to come back to Capstone for my second book – a decision I am very pleased I made. She is a prime example of having empathy – in her case, for authors.

Morag Cuddeford-Jones who has the equivalent of a silver pen for writing and has helped me write, shape and structure a book that was just a stream of consciousness at the beginning.

Once the writing was over, the swot team who have turned around a Microsoft Word document and made it into this book are the very switched-on team at Capstone who have been a pleasure to work with: especially: Grace O'Byrne, Megan Varilly, Caroline Baines, Emma Knott and Jenny Ng.

There are many who have nudged this book forward: Jason Dunne for guiding me through the publishing process from an insider's perspective; Lupus von Maltzahn for helping me with the backbone and soul of this book; Brendan O' Connor for being a great sounding board to bounce ideas.

This book has come about from my speaking career so I owe thanks to my speaker agents for giving me the opportunity, and to all the companies who have invited me to speak and who have shared their frustrations and aspirations with me giving me so much food for thought.

Also available from **Capstone**

ISBN: 9781906465537

ISBN: 9781906465827

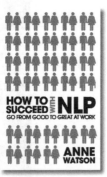

ISBN: 9781907293054

ISBN: 9781907293047

ISBN: 9781906465421

ISBN: 9781906465582